PROFUMO

PROFUMO

The Hate Factor

David Thurlow

ROBERT HALE · LONDON

ISBN 0 7090 4750 9

Robert Hale Limited
Clerkenwell House
Clerkenwell Green
London EC1R 0HT

Photoset in Ehrhardt by
Derek Doyle & Associates, Mold, Clwyd.
Printed in Great Britain by
St Edmundsbury Press Ltd, Bury St Edmunds, Suffolk.
Bound by Hunter & Foulis Ltd.

CONTENTS

List of Illustrations   6
Acknowledgements   7
Introduction   8

1 John Lewis   10
2 First Libel   16
3 Privilege   20
4 Stephen Ward   28
5 The Mullally Libel Case   35
6 Divorce   46
7 The Fifties   55
8 Profumo and Keeler   62
9 The Lewis Libel Case   72
10 Time Lag   79
11 1962   85
12 The Shooting   96
13 Out in the Open   103
14 The Snowball Rolls On   127
15 Avalanche   143
16 The End of the Affair   159
17 Victory for Lewis   170
18 Conclusion   183

Sources   187
Bibliography   188
Index   189

ILLUSTRATIONS

Between pages 96 and 97

1 Mandy Rice-Davies and Christine Keeler at the height of the scandal
2 Lucky Gordon outside Marylebone Court in October 1963
3 The prosecutor, Mervyn Griffith-Jones, in the Ward trial
4 James Burge, the man who defended Stephen Ward
5 The Russian Naval Attaché spy, Captain Eugene Ivanov
6 Stephen Ward leaving the Old Bailey in cheerful mood
7 Mandy Rice-Davies on a high in December 1963
8 Paymaster-General George Wigg
9 Lord 'Bill' Astor – Ward's landlord and patient
10 Profumo arrives home after confessing to his wife
11 Lord Denning about to start on his report
12 Stephen Ward arriving at the Old Bailey
13 Lewis in the sixties at the time of his great triumph
14 Macmillan with his wife

PICTURE CREDITS

All the illustrations are reproduced with the kind permission of *The Times*.

ACKNOWLEDGEMENTS

Many of those who could have helped with this book are dead. Others chose, as is their right, not to help at all, but many did, particularly Freddy Mullally, Caroline Kennedy, Eddie Chapman, Phillip Knightley, Roy East and R. Barry O'Brien.

I would like to thank my colleagues in *The Times* archives and picture libraries, particularly Stan Cummins-Stanley, Dick Ibbott and Mick Roffey, for their great help, and *The Times* for permission to use court and parliamentary reports from 1946 to 1964 and to reproduce their photographs. I am very grateful. There are many books and articles on the Profumo Affair and the events surrounding it. I have used the Denning Report as the official guide for dates and fixing events.

The book is dedicated to Jeanne

INTRODUCTION

When Lord Denning sat down in the late summer of 1963 to write his report on the Profumo Affair– the biggest political scandal this century, which finished the careers of Profumo, the Minister of War, and of Harold Macmillan, the Prime Minister, and was to lead to the defeat of the Tory government after thirteen years – he said that the story must start with Stephen Ward, osteopath, sketcher of royals, leading politicians and top people, and provider of popsies to his rich and influential friends.

Denning was wrong.

The story began eleven years earlier, in 1952, because a man called John Lewis believed wrongly that Ward had slept with his wife; he vowed vengeance, a threat to be taken extremely seriously when made by Lewis.

Lewis had a fatal flaw in his character. He was a former Labour MP, a successful businessman, an inventor responsible for some of the rubber substitutes so vital for the national survival in the Second World War, a racehorse owner and socialite. He and his wife Joy, sixteen years younger and a Jewish princess, mixed in the swinging set of those days.

But hidden behind his suave front was the flaw: such was the intensity of his sexual jealousy that it overrode any normal thinking. He was bad enough about any slight. He would seek vengeance without thinking of the cost, as on the occasion when he took a neighbour at the block of luxury flats in St. John's Wood where he lived to the High Court in a minor row over a badly parked car.

When it came to sex, his hatred, and his obsession with seeing the focus of his hatred destroyed, was overwhelming. He would wake each morning thinking of a new way in which he could harm the object of his hate.

And so it was in 1952 when he was convinced – and nothing

8

anyone could say would dissuade him from his belief – that Ward, one of the swinging set, had slept with Joy that the pathological hatred began. In fact, they had only talked when she ran out of her home after a row with her husband. Lewis, who had a taste for prostitutes, could not accept that a man and a woman could talk and nothing else. He judged everyone by the way he behaved.

From that moment Lewis was determined to punish Ward severely. He rang the police and inland revenue anonymously to give them false tips about Ward's activities, and informed newspaper contacts.

However, it was not until he met a long-legged nymphet called Christine Keeler at a Christmas party in 1962, ten years later, and she began to talk that he had the ammunition to fix Ward for ever. She had no idea who Lewis was, but that meeting was responsible for the Profumo Affair becoming public, even though it was all over fifteen months before they met.

Lewis and Lewis alone was responsible and this is the story of the man, his career as an MP, his clashes with the law, his vicious divorce, his High Court litigation, his record libel damages in 1961, his character and the events that led up to the Profumo Affair. It is the story of how he set the snowball rolling and kept pushing once it was in motion.

For thirty years I have read every book, article and report I could find about the Profumo Affair and have spoken to many people. From time to time there has been a reference to Lewis, but it has not been developed. Rarely in political autobiographies and biographies of the time did I find his name and if he was mentioned, it was in passing.

At the same time, there was the puzzling problem of the nineteen-month time lag between the end of the Affair and the uproar and disaster which occurred in the summer of 1963. It never made any sense until I started enquiring about Lewis.

The answer to why the Affair became public and why there was a time lag was the same: John Lewis. Without him if it had ever come out it would have been the word of a girl who shared her favours from the highest and then downwards and who enjoyed mild drugs, against that of a respected senior politician and potential prime minister. Whom would the press believe and would they risk it anyway?

Enter Lewis and all is clear.

1
JOHN LEWIS

John Lewis was born just before the First World War, the eldest son in a middle-class Jewish family. His father was a clever man, inventing rubber processes for use in industry, a skill John maintained, particularly during the war when the family company, Rubber Improvement Ltd, was responsible in a large part for the production of tyres for bombers. After the war, John, as chairman and managing director, moved into the field of rubber conveyor belts for the coal industry and at one time was by far the largest supplier.

He went to Grocers' school and later the City of London College, and trained to be a rubber technologist; he used his knowledge to become an inventor. He was joint inventor of a rubber substitute for cable and general rubber production.

He was brought up in the large north London area where all the leading Jewish families live and began his political life by joining the Labour party League of Youth in 1928. Before the war he stood in local borough elections without success, but all the time he was gaining experience. He was known as an enthusiastic if arrogant and pompous young man, going places and keen to get to the top in life and politics. He stayed an active socialist all his life, and in 1950, when standing for re-election in Bolton where he was the sitting member, he wrote in his manifesto: 'I am a supporter of fundamental Labour policy. I believe that greater national production can be secured by increased incentives to workers obtainable by the adjustment of fiscal policy to allow for differentation in the rate of income tax or exemption from income tax in respect of overtime payments.' Good common-sense stuff. By that time he was employing over two thousand people in London and the east Midlands at his two factories, and he knew what he was talking about.

Lewis was accepted but not greatly liked outside his own family circle. Like many Jewish young men in his social stratum he did not rush into marriage. As a young man he had many girl-friends, but they did not fit his idea of a wife.

During the war not only did his firm in Willesden produce essential goods for the war effort, but Lewis himself was an adviser to the first rubber controller in the Ministry of Supply. There was no rubber coming into Britain because of the Japanese invasion of Malaya which had cut off all supplies. Nearly all our rubber came from there, and Lewis and others like him had to produce a substitute which could really work. He was also consultant to the Ministry of Economic Warfare. Lewis's special ability lay in the production of reclaimed rubber and rubber substitutes including elasticized asphalt. His was a valuable contribution.

In 1944 he was selected as one of the Labour prospective candidates for the two Bolton seats and was comfortably elected in the Attlee landslide which followed the Second World War.

Lewis went into the House of Commons and revelled in it. He was a good MP, mixed well and was very popular in the Lancashire cotton town. He was out and about, always ready to see a constituent and deal with any problem. He was still a bachelor, but reaching the time when he would marry.

His name was first noticed after the Bolton football disaster in 1946. On 9 March thirty-three fans were killed and a further five hundred seriously injured when steel barriers collapsed at the Wanderers' ground. It happened when thousands of eager fans tried to get into the ground to see the cup tie against Stoke City (for whom the great Stanley Matthews was playing). They pulled down fencing to get into an already packed enclosure.

The police had closed the entrance gates an hour before the surge. But the fans, not unlike those at Hillsborough in the late eighties, were determined. They overwhelmed the police and kept moving on into an impossible situation. They broke down the perimeter fencing and a human mass converged on the crowd already inside. Several fans were crushed to death and a greater disaster was averted only by the prompt action of the police who, from the pitch, ripped down the fencing around it so that hundreds of people spilled on to the field and did not die.

After the tragedy Lewis, years ahead of his time, pressed for a conference between the Football League and the Football Association to arrange consultation with clubs with a view to agreeing safe maximum attendances. In the light of what was to happen in the Sheffield disaster four decades later, the reply of the then Home Secretary, Chuter Ede, is interesting. He said:

> The number of people who could be safely admitted depends so largely on the individual circumstances of the ground that I doubt whether it would be useful to attempt to deal with the question centrally.
>
> Pending further consideration of the machinery necessary for determining and enforcing maximum safety attendances I am sure that the clubs will take every precaution open to them and in this connection will study the report on the Bolton disaster.

A few weeks later Lewis was in the limelight again. In those days newspapers were very thin because of the shortage of paper, and politicians did not get the massive coverage and publicity they do today. In May, 263 paratroopers from the 13th Battalion (Lancashire) Parachute Regiment, many from the Bolton area, were charged with mutiny. They were veterans of the D-Day landings as part of the 6th Airborne Division, fighting in the Ardennes and crossing the Rhine before being transferred to south-east Asia with the reoccupation troops after the Japanese surrender; they had then seen action in Java.

They came out of the jungle in Malaya and went from camp to camp, where the conditions were appalling. Finally, at Muar, they had had enough. There was one tent and three taps for three hundred men and not a shower in sight; when it rained the camp became a sea of mud. They may have come from two-up, two-downs in mean streets in Lancashire, but at home there was warmth and food and fun. They were learning that fighting for your country meant living in disgusting conditions. They held a meeting and subsequently refused to fall in, so they were arrested and charged.

It was clear that the Army wanted a show trial to discourage the others. Lewis took an active interest from the start but it was Tom Driberg, a fellow MP, renowned for his homosexual activities and saved from gaol only by his friends in high places, who raised the question for the first time in the House of Commons. He asked the War Minister if he knew that the men were being detained in 'acute conditions of overcrowding in nine rooms'. The minister waffled his way out of that one.

However, the new MP for Bolton wanted to see for himself what was going on and flew out at his own expense, giving up his holiday, to the court martial, held in a tent the size of a circus marquee by an airstrip at Kluang, sixty miles from Singapore.

There was not much Lewis could do in the stifling heat amongst heavy military legal brass who were determined to make an example of these men. The weight of evidence against them was slightly tempered by their own commanding officer, who told how the Muar camp was the fourth billet in succession where the conditions for the men were bad. At one camp there had been no beds, no water and a single tent for all of them.

It made little difference. Lewis had to go home long before the trial ended. It did so with twenty acquittals. Of the remaining 243 men, eight were given five years and the rest three years, all with hard labour, and were ordered to be discharged with ignominy. On review all sentences were reduced to two years' hard labour and discharge.

Lewis went into action to make sure that the men did not serve their sentences and were not booted out of the Army. His campaign was helped by the knowledge that the commander-in-chief in the area had said that the men need not go back to Britain to serve their sentences and had given a general nod that the sentences could be reviewed at any time. The men went back to their units, not into prison or to do hard labour, and knew that as long as they behaved themselves they would not have to do their time. In effect they had been reprieved, although no public announcement was made.

A lot of work went on behind the scenes, with Lewis at the front. He not only pressed for their release, backed by a petition of 100,000 signatures from Lancashire and Yorkshire, but also demanded that the officers who had been responsible for allowing such terrible conditions should be court-martialled too.

He said in the House: 'It is the duty of the government to take action against these bad officers who were responsible for what took place. One cannot condone mutiny. But what conditions existed to make some of the most highly disciplined troops in the world protest in this way?'

Although nothing happened, he was on a winner, his first, and it made his name in Lancashire.

The next year he announced his engagement to Joy Jocille Fletcher, daughter of a wealthy north London builder, Horace Fletcher. She was eighteen and a wonderful catch. The announcement made the national press and there was a photograph of Joy. In Bolton there were many congratulations for the new MP. Not only was he doing much for his constituents, but his business acumen was admired as well. As memories of the war stood strong in everyone's mind, more and more details of who did what were emerging. It was very much in Lewis's favour that he was one of the leaders in the field of rubber substitutes and had been using them for cables and tyres for the services, a vital ingredient in the war effort.

He had also made a name for leading the attack on the Boxing Board of Control for their colour bar on champions. This led to the ban being lifted and opened the way for men like the Turpin brothers to go for British titles, and for Randy Turpin to win the world crown from Sugar Ray Robinson. Lewis had also become a freeman and liveryman of the Carmen Company.

The wedding was a great Jewish social affair at the Hampstead synagogue on 17 February, 1948. Joy, a superb Jewish princess in a beautiful wedding gown with a trailing veil, looked stupendous as she was given away by her father. Lewis, a carnation in the buttonhole of his tailcoat, appeared extremely affluent. He was thirty-five, rich, and slightly balding. She was nineteen, an heiress and extremely attractive. They made a handsome pair as they cut the four-tier cake at the reception where dozens gathered to toast their future.

What the pictures do not show and what Joy did not know was her husband's true character. His sexual preferences and way of life might not be everyone's taste, but many are like that. What was to take Lewis out of the ordinary was his incredible sexual jealousy and his powers of revenge. It was not until he suspected Joy of being unfaithful, although he was unfaithful as a matter of course, that this side of his character began to show.

Once it had been planted, the seed grew in his mind and he could never ignore it. He was prepared to keep at it, an obsession that most do not have the stamina for, because hatred dies away and it takes a heavy prod to reactivate it. But in Lewis's case it was a daily waking passion, a loathing and determination to get the object of his hatred, whatever happened.

A close friend said after his death: 'There is no more powerful passion than sexual jealousy. It is overpowering, overriding everything in its intensity. People kill for it. In John's case it burnt deep and long inside him and he swore vengeance. And when John swore vengeance he meant it whatever the cost, however long.'

This passion did not appear until four years into his marriage but before then there had been a hint that he was not a man to cross, because he would take the matter to the furthest possible adjudication. He thrived on litigation and hatred, as many were to find to their cost.

2

FIRST LIBEL

By 1949 Lewis was doing well. He was married, with prospects
of wealth to come from his own company and from his wife's
family business. He was chairman of the Empire Games 1950
appeal committee to raise funds for the games in Auckland,
New Zealand. He was keen on all manner of sports, being
organizer of the National Coal Board boxing championships and
a steward of the British Boxing Board of Control. He was
chairman of the House of Commons all-party motor club, a
member of the Amateur Athletic Association and a vice-
president of his constituency's athletic club, Bolton United
Harriers, whose top runners included international champion
Geoffrey Saunders and world-record breaking long-distance
runner Fred Norris.

Lewis, a Fabian, was doing well in the House too. He was on
the Select Committee for Estimates and the Parliamentary and
Scientific Committee. As his own business prospered under his
skilful guidance and because of his powers of invention, he was
able to offer advice to fellow MPs on business; he also made his
mark as one of the pioneers for the extension of television
services.

In March 1949 Lewis made news twice. Three weeks before
the Budget, Lewis asked John Edwards, the parliamentary
secretary to the Board of Trade, to do away with price control
for boots and shoes so that they would be cheaper. It was an
important question and he was cheered by MPs from both sides.

But the cheers fell on deaf ears. Edwards did not agree that
price controls were responsible for higher profits than usual. He
shook his head when Lewis insisted: 'Prices will fall if you take
away the control.'

Edwards retorted: 'It will be maintained until we are satisfied
that it can be removed without risk of people having to pay more

for their boots and shoes.'

It was a classic reply, and Lewis had to take it.

A few days later Lewis was in the papers again, this time while on a visit to his constituency, where he was an increasingly popular member. He toured the Townley hospital just outside the Lancashire cotton town and twenty minutes later was back in as a patient. He met the daughter of a friend on her horse near the hospital. Lewis gave the horse a pat and it replied by giving him a hefty kick in the leg. He had to return to the hospital for treatment for a severe gash.

A few months later he showed in public for the first time the vindictive streak in his nature, the obsession that was to bring about his downfall and in turn the downfall of everyone who crossed him. He could not leave things alone.

This obsession led to his first visit to the courts to sue someone. To those in the House of Commons who knew him as a hard-working member who looked after his constituents well, who made sensible speeches and suggestions, had held junior office under the Postmaster General, who was affable if arrogant, it came as a shock. It revealed a side of his character that they did not know. Those more shrewd, the party leaders and those who advised them, were also surprised. They were not so surprised later when Lewis became more and more vicious in pursuing actions. But this was the first public airing of what was to become a common practice. This is not to say that he was wrong to sue in later cases. He often won, but he scored victories on occasions when others would not have gone after a quarry with such venom. Most thought some of his personal actions were not of the sort that should have been put through the courts and given the extensive publicity which they received because of Lewis's position and the legal luminaries involved.

The case in the High Court was almost petty. Indeed, one counsel described it as 'a storm in a teacup', although he was implying that it was the effects of drinking from an alcoholic cup that had caused the trouble.

The barrister who made this allegation was Gerald Gardiner, KC, who later became Lord Chancellor. Lewis was represented by Reginald Paget, KC, a Labour MP and acquaintance of his. The judge was Mr Justice Hallett, a tough nut of the old school who had the kind of voice that John Mortimer describes as sounding like parchment cracking.

The case lasted two days and involved an allegation by Lewis that he had been slandered by a neighbour of his in Abbey Lodge, St John's Wood, where he had a luxurious ground-floor flat. It was alleged that the neighbour had said that Lewis was not sober, an allegation the neighbour strongly denied.

Paget, for Lewis, said that in March 1948, fourteen months earlier, the neighbour found he could not open a door of his car because Lewis's Rolls Royce was parked in such a way that it was impossible to do so. The neighbour got in a rage and declared:

'Whoever parked this car ought to have driving lessons.'

When he was told that Lewis owned the car and had parked it he said:

'He could not have been sober.'

A little later, in front of Lewis, his chauffeur and the superintendent of the block of luxury flats, he said: 'He must have been drunk.'

Lewis was asked by Gerald Gardiner why he had brought the action. Lewis was adamant. He said: 'An allegation was made against me. All I wanted was an apology but one was not forthcoming.'

The KC pressed on. 'Did you apologize for leaving your car as you did?'

'Oh no,' said Lewis. 'No apology was due in the circumstances. I took a serious view of the allegation and wished to get it withdrawn.'

Over forty years later it is almost impossible to believe that someone would have sued over such a small incident. Consider the cost of having two (then) King's Counsel with juniors for two days in the High Court because someone in a temper had said that you must have been drunk to park your car in such a way. Think of having the affair dragged out over fourteen months before it came to court, the legal bills for consultation with solicitors, the briefing of and conferences with barristers. It beggars belief if you did not know the man. In those days very few knew the man and what he was capable of.

Lewis was followed into the witness box by his chauffeur Charles, who told the judge that he thought that when the neighbour said Lewis must have been drunk, the charge was made seriously.

Gardiner suggested the word 'drunk' was never used, but Charles insisted it was.

Gardiner then opened his case for the neighbour, telling the jury that they had to decide whether the words were spoken, whether, if they had been, they were to be taken seriously, and whether they would be understood as imputing that Lewis had committed a criminal offence.

The neighbour's defence was that he had not alleged that Lewis was drunk.

He explained what had happened. He said that the cars were touching and it was impossible for him to get to the nearside of his car. He said that he was annoyed, but had not said that Lewis was drunk.

He emphasized this. 'I did not use the word drunk and I never intended to suggest that Lewis was drunk. I thought the car had been parked in a selfish and inconsiderate way.'

It was a reasonable thing to think. The incident happened when he called on Lewis to move so that he could open the nearside door of his car. Lewis was annoyed. But instead of leaving the matter once it had been sorted out, he resorted to the law at the very highest level. The neighbour must have been astonished to find that what was a very minor incident was becoming a case in one of the highest courts in the land, with the man accusing him of slander determined to go all the way without a care for the cost.

Luckily for the neighbour he did not have to pay. In their closing speeches both counsel listed the pros and cons but Gardiner made the most telling point, that it was 'a storm in a teacup'. The jury thought so too, and found for the neighbour. The judge made an order that Lewis should pay the costs.

The publicity did Lewis no good. It puzzled his friends and was noted by those who ran the Labour party.

Everyone who had dealings with Lewis should have had this incident etched strongly in their memories because it was the first inkling of what he was like. Human nature being what it is, those actively involved with him forgot it except in moments when they were talking in passing about his character. They were wrong to let it pass. It showed what he was capable of when roused. He must have known that it was a stupid case to bring, an action that he would not only probably lose but which would make him a laughing stock. For a man of his arrogance and self-importance, that was something he did not want.

But he still went ahead. It was the first flake of the snowball.

3

PRIVILEGE

By the summer of 1951 Lewis was a favourite MP with his constituents but had fallen foul of those in power in the Labour party, which was still in government. Those shrewd enough to watch knew of his gambling, his unscrupulous business methods, his womanizing and night-clubbing. They realized that he was not an asset to the party and could cause them embarrassment at some stage.

Lewis was a happy man, often out and about at night with his wife, mixing at the edge of a social set that included in those years Baron, the photographer, the Marquis of Milford Haven and his friend the Duke of Edinburgh, who as Prince Philip, was one of the crowd until his marriage to Princess Elizabeth. Among Lewis's new friends was Dr Stephen Ward, a smooth, fast-talking and handsome osteopath who was also a very talented artist. He drew his friends, and his sketches were highly sought. He was always surrounded by pretty girls – lovely girls, some available for sex, others just highly attractive and nice. Stephen attracted girls like a honey pot attracts wasps and bees. He was always cheerful, full of fun and excitement and was one of a social crowd which Lewis envied and wanted to join. He did.

But that summer Lewis again showed his colleagues and friends how he reacted when crossed. He did so, which made it worse for him, in the House of Commons, where the Prime Minister Clem Attlee and others on the front bench were not among his fans.

It happened because John Lewis, MP, had to show two young policemen in the rush hour just how important he was. The traffic was very heavy as he drove to the House of Commons for a three-line Whip on an Argentinian meat agreement. He planned to take his usual route along Bayswater Road and through Victoria Gate in Hyde Park and across to Westminster. He was held up at Victoria Gate, which is some way from the House of Commons. He had to be at the House by seven o'clock and the minutes were passing. We can imagine how he fumed and cursed. He was not a patient man.

There were two versions of what happened next. Lewis arrived late and immediately complained to the Speaker that he had been held up and diverted; he wanted a ruling on whether it was a case of breach of privilege. In the furore that followed – and it was a big one – Winston Churchill, Aneurin Bevan, Chuter Ede, the Home Secretary, Reginald Paget and other leading names of the day all had a say. It was that he had been obstructed by the police on his way to the House and had been served with summonses in connection with the incident.

The other version was given by the police when the case came to court and it puts the matter in context to relate this before describing what happened in the House.

Lewis, after an adjournment because he was on holiday, appeared at Marylebone magistrates' court on 26 September, nearly three months after the original incident on 3 July, to plead guilty to driving without reasonable consideration and failing to stop at the request of a police officer at the Victoria Gate entrance to Hyde Park from Bayswater Road.

The stipendiary magistrate, Mr Rowland Thomas, QC, heard that the traffic was very heavy, that Lewis queue-jumped from fifth position to the front and was stopped by the police. He told the policeman that he was a member of parliament and asked to be let through the gate.

The policeman suggested that he went along to the Marble Arch entrance to the park. Lewis was extremely angry and kept revving up his engine and twice his bumper touched the policeman's legs.

Eventually, as tempers rose on both sides, the traffic cleared and Lewis was able to go on. Instead, he said it was too late.

Mr John Bass, prosecuting, said that when Lewis was asked if he had seen the signal, he replied: 'Of course I saw your signal but I am in far too much of a hurry to worry about that.'

The angry MP told the constable that he was going to report the matter to the Speaker.

John Busse, for Lewis, said that he had received a three-line Whip ordering him to be at the House for the division. The Labour majority in that parliament was just eight. Busse went on: 'Lewis took the view that the constable was not as helpful as he might have been and as his orders required him to be.

'Temper naturally rose on both sides. If the constable had had perhaps more experience – he had only been twelve months in the Metropolitan police – and if Lewis had not been under such a compulsion to get to the House, this incident would never have arisen.'

Lewis, he said, was exceedingly angry. He put his car into gear and revved up to move forward as soon as possible. It might well be that his bumper did twice touch the constable but: 'No-one but a lunatic would drive a motor car deliberately in to the back of a police constable while he was doing his duty.'

Fining him four pounds with ten guineas' costs – a third charge of obstructing police was not proceeded with – the magistrate said:

'I have no doubt that Mr Lewis got angry. I can find nothing at all on the part of the officers which deserves criticism of any sort or kind.

'I believe a little more patience on the part of Mr Lewis would have prevented this trouble and he now probably appreciates it.

'Members of parliament have no greater right at that spot than ordinary members of the public. I think the officers did all they could for him and in fact assisted him and gave him advice to enable him to get to the House of Commons.'

Nothing, he said, was more likely to cause confusion to the police who were trying to control traffic at the gate, which was difficult to negotiate, than to have someone come out of the line of traffic and jump the queue.

It was typical of Lewis that he should try to use his position as an MP to take precedence over other drivers. It was not as if he was close to the House. He had to get through Hyde Park and then round Parliament Square. If he had been in Parliament Square it would have been a different matter. If he had stopped a policeman and explained that he had to be in the House to vote, he would have understood.

But Lewis, arrogant and very much impressed with his own importance, showed that trait in his character, possibly due to his upbringing as favoured son, which made him always insist he was right, that he should have his way and heaven help those who did anything to stop him.

The constables were little men to be jumped on by Mr John Lewis, MP. Later, when people crossed him over much bigger issues he behaved in the same fashion. His character was such that he saw a slight as an insult to be pursued to infinite lengths.

To go back to 3 July, the day of the incident, and the House of Commons. We can imagine that Lewis, having parked his Rolls Royce, was bursting with fury at being late, being stopped and having his dignity as an MP pricked. He must have given vent to his anger to the Speaker.

The timetable after that is important. On 14 July Lewis received statutory notice from the police in a document dated the day before, the thirteenth, of their intention to prosecute him over the incident at Victoria Gate. Two days later, on the sixteenth, he tabled a motion in the House asking for a select committee to be set up to inquire into his obstruction by the police. Two days later, on the eighteenth, he received three summonses in the post, dated the day before.

So Lewis took no action until he received the notice of intent to prosecute him. This fact was not lost on some MPs, who were not pleased. Others, Labour colleagues such as Reginald Paget and Sydney Silverman, supported him over his dignity as a member of parliament and his right to be aided by the police to get to the House on time.

So, on 24 July, Lewis was on his feet to ask the Speaker to rule as to whether there was a prima facie case of breach of privilege by the police action which had affected him. Nye Bevan and Winston Churchill who were mighty foes, both spoke in the short debate which ended with a Committee of Privileges being set up after the members had outvoted the Speaker's decision that there had been no breach.

The Speaker said that privilege did not protect members against the service of summonses and a member could not prevent the police from prosecuting him for alleged motoring offences by putting a notice of motion on the order paper. This brought cheering, because many of the members saw what Lewis was up to. The Speaker also said that he had not advised Lewis to put down the motion – which Lewis said he had – but had told him that this was the only way to raise the matter. This caused one of the sponsors of the motion, Earl Winterton, who had accepted what Lewis had told him, to take his name off the motion.

Then Sydney Silverman, a great campaigner for the abolition of capital punishment, said that the question of whether the police obstructed the member or the member obstructed the police was a matter for the House to consider if privilege was involved. Conflict between the courts and parliament could only be avoided if the issue was determined in the House, not in a court.

Mr Paget, a Labour KC who appeared for Lewis in the courts, said that an inferior court (meaning the magistrates), should not start proceedings when a superior court (meaning the House), was considering the matter. But one of the Tory backbenchers made the reasonable point that Lewis had been told by the police of their intention to summons him before he put the motion on the order paper. Another Tory backbencher made a similar point. He said: 'I believe it is contrary to the interests of this House that we should even appear to make the novel claim that a member is in any way immune from the ordinary process of criminal justice.'

Although the Speaker then said he was not changing his mind, Mr Silverman pressed on for a vote. He said: 'The simple question is whether a member was obstructing a policeman in the course of a policeman's duty or whether the policeman was obstructing the member in the exercise of a privilege.'

Mr Paget put it in legal terms. He said: 'If I tried to enter this House by Palace Yard and a policeman tried to stop me and I pushed by, either I was right because of my privilege or I have committed the offence of obstructing the policeman in the course of his duty.' He went on to say that the very thing on which the magistrate was being asked to adjudicate was an assertion – rightly or wrongly – of privilege and the House of Commons was the judge of its own privileges.

Weighty stuff. Lewis sat there preening himself, the centre of attention.

What Paget had said was valid but there was one difference: being given priority in the Palace Yard or even Parliament Square was one thing; expecting the same thing in a traffic jam the other side of Hyde Park and a mile or so away was quite another.

The Committee of Privileges met and took evidence from

Lewis and the policeman. They threw out Lewis's complaint. They said: 'If the service of the summonses in these circumstances were to constitute a breach of privilege, then a member could protect himself against any service of process for criminal acts by placing a motion on the order paper.' In other words do not hide behind your membership of the Commons if you have broken the law and want to avoid the courts.

The report continued: 'In any case because a member or members have tabled a motion it does not follow that such a motion will be considered by the House. The order paper has no legal significance and motions placed thereupon do not bring their matters within the scope of *sub judice* proceedings.' It went on to say that there was no obstruction or delay by either of the policemen concerned and that no breach of privilege was caused by them. It ruled that no breach of privilege was involved by the issue of the summons. The report also said that both policemen recognized the House of Commons badge on the car and knew that MPs should not be delayed but should have free and uninterrupted passage; the committee were satisfied that neither wanted to delay Lewis, and both were in fact anxious to assist him. If they had not been, they would have detained him on his way while they took full particulars of his name, address, driving licence and insurance certificate.

There was no attempt to delay Lewis deliberately. Far from obstructing him, the police behaved reasonably and sensibly and did all they could to help him get to the Commons (for a division which in the end never took place. It was all in vain).

The committee reported on the conflict of evidence between the MP and one of the policemen, PC Cordingley, who was not called to speak in court because of Lewis's guilty plea. Cordingley told them: 'I stood in front of his car and held my left arm out as a signal to stop. He then ran his car into the back of me. I stepped forward and he ran his car into me again. He did it a third time, only this time he kept moving his car slowly forward, pushing me along with it.'

We can just imagine this angry, arrogant man, always used to having his own way, dealing with the presumptuous young constable, wet behind the ears, in new uniform fresh from college, by pushing him along with the bumper of his Rolls. It is another clue to his character: here is a man who always wants his own way, even when the problem is one of his own making.

PC Cordingley went on: 'I walked round towards Mr Lewis and as I was walking round towards the offside of his car he shot through the park.'

Lewis naturally denied all this. If he had touched the officer it was an accident on a slight hill where the car was moving backwards and forwards with the clutch out, he asserted. He said: 'If he was leaning against the car, from what you say, he might have felt a movement. But the clutch was not let out when he was there and there was no move forward.'

The committee also consulted Erskine May, the parliamentary authority and bible on the question of privilege. It said that it was a breach of privilege to molest a member anywhere, while attending the Commons or going to or from it.

However, the Speaker had ruled back in 1937 that the passage in Erskine May stating that 'passages through the streets leading to the House be kept free and open' referred to the neighbourhood of the House and that the Victoria Gate in Hyde Park was not a street within the meaning of the Order.

When the report was considered by the House later that day Lewis got up to do the only thing he could do, and it came hard to him: he apologized. He said;

I would ask the House to accept that whatever occurred on the night of 3 July arose out of my natural anxiety to get to the House for what I believed to be a critical division.

I think on reflection it was unwise for me to have reported this matter at the time to the Speaker but I believed that that was the proper course to take. For whatever action taken subsequently I want to assure the House it was taken on the best advice available to me.

At the time the incident occurred I was extremely agitated because I thought I would not get to the House in time. When one is in a state of nervous anxiety tempers are likely to get frayed and if this condition contributed in any way to the difficulties that arose I can only express my regrets.

I do not propose to say anything about the evidence given to the committee except to say that the evidence I gave was true.

There was some discussion and Mr Paget made two points: that a man who did not like the Labour party had told him that he had seen the incident and there was no traffic obstruction, and that he agreed with a leader in *The Times* that day deploring frivolous complaints of privilege. Members should be careful not to be touchy about their rights and not be assertive.

He was not complaining directly about Lewis because he said the committee had gone outside their function in trying the issue, rejecting Lewis's evidence on some points against that of the police and prejudicing the trial. Other MPs spoke and at the end the committee's report was accepted.

It is interesting that in the next debate that day, which was also about privilege in quite a different connection, one of the speakers was the Labour MP for Dudley, George Wigg, a tall man with a big nose useful for sniffing out information. He and Lewis knew each other as racing fans and often met at racecourses. Their acquaintanceship later became a formidable dagger to thrust into the heart of the government.

Lewis was not happy about the outcome. The truth was that he had been made to look a fool. A normal MP, even though his dignity had been damaged a little by the delay, would not have allowed himself to get into such a position by losing his temper, and would have let the matter drop. He might have told his friends about it, as people do when they have a slight brush with the law. He might have said that the police were very reasonable in the end and let him go on as quickly as they could. It was a nuisance that he was late, but really it was his fault and he would have shaken his head at his stupidity.

Not Lewis. He was a clever, astute man but with this flaw. With some he could bully and push and get his way, make his will obeyed, carry on his vendetta. But in the House of Commons he was up against some of the cleverest minds in the country and they saw through him.

Later that year he lost his seat and never won it back.

4

STEPHEN WARD

After the privilege case, other MPs in general and party leaders in particular watched Lewis more carefully. His attempts to get contracts by not quite scrupulous means were noted. He was so eager at the Board of Trade, where Harold Wilson was in charge, that he was barred from the building. Wilson and his senior civil servants did not like their junior staff being offered bribes by a man looking for major contracts with the Coal Board for rubber conveyor belts. They also learnt that union officers were at Lewis's parties, which were rich and swell affairs with cinema and theatre stars, journalists and swinging people of that era. They were fun. His social life improved as his political career suffered. He lost his seat in the 1951 election when the Tories got back into power for the first time since the war. Lewis was defeated by a Liberal who was in league with the Tories in the two Bolton seats: the Tories and Liberals had agreed not to fight each other, thereby crushing the Labour vote.

Lewis admired Stephen Ward and he and his wife were in the circle that met at Paddy Kennedy's pub, The Star in Belgravia, and then moved on to restaurants and clubs for dinner and then to dance the night away. There were several bachelors in the crowd and some names were to become very famous.

But the great attraction of the group in those austere days of shortages and post-war blues were that they had a great deal of fun, drinking, dining and fornicating. Everyone ended up in bed, married couples nearly always together, but there was much more class and style about everything than in the swinging sixties. Freddy Mullally, a great friend of Lewis until he too crossed him – and it was an accusation that Freddy, editor, publicist, journalist and international author, denied then and does to this day – remembers particularly that the women were always well turned out. It was a moment to look forward to at the end of the day when the men in evening dress or very smart lounge suits gathered in The Star, waiting for the ladies to turn up. When they did they looked fabulous. Kay Kendall and her sister were among the beautiful women, supremely groomed.

Ward always arrived with a girl or two on his arm. He could attract them with his mellifluous voice which seemed to tell each of them that she was the most special girl in the world. He could seduce them into bed with his voice. He treated girls in a way they liked. Lewis, who did not have that social smoothness, envied him.

In those heady days of the new decade Ward was riding very high indeed. It was another ten years before he began to descend the sexual ladder towards easy girls, drugs and later seedy prostitutes he plucked off the street – at the same time as he was still mixing in high circles with top men and very smooth beautiful girls.

Ward was the son of a country parson who had livings in Lemsford, near Hatfield, Hertfordshire, and then in Twickenham, Torquay and Rochester while Stephen was growing up. Later he was abroad, flitting home occasionally when he was back in the country. Ward was reticent about his childhood in later life when his charm and suave sophistication were supreme, but there was a moment at his public school which may explain his predilection for sexual perversions. It certainly explains why, when he was cornered in the last few days of his life, locked in a cell on remand and knowing he was going to face imprisonment and disgrace, he did not open his mouth and sing all he knew about the behaviour and the morals of those in high places who would have done anything to keep him quiet. They did not need to because Stephen Ward was no sneak. He knew the code. He took his punishment like a man and did not tell on the others.

It happened in the dormitory one night when he was in his early teens. Two boys were romping about and one, in the dark, was hit and fell unconscious. He recovered after being taken to the sanatorium and the next day there was an inquiry to find out who was responsible. As was traditional in public schools then, no-one said a word. If the chap who did it was not prepared to own up, then he was a cad and a blaggard but no-one would point a finger at him. The boys would take revenge later, but in their own time.

So it happened that Ward was chosen to be the sacrifice, for the first of only two occasions in his life. He was suspected by the housemaster and although he was in fact innocent, he was selected to be punished. It was the usual retribution: stinging cuts of the cane as he knelt spread-eagled over a chair, with only thin pyjamas to protect his burning buttocks, and the whole school there to watch. Ward took his beating like a man, just like he was expected to do, fighting back the tears as he took each cut and felt the bite nip into his flesh. When it was over he stood, put his dressing-gown back on and walked from the hall. Every eye was on him to see how he had taken it, watching to see a hint of a tear, each ear strained for a cry of pain, and each boy thankful it was not him. One was especially thankful that he had escaped because he had kept his mouth shut. Now that fool Ward was having his backside thrashed instead of him.

Ward did not let down the side, did not break the code, had not snitched, had taken the punishment and was admired for his pluck, courage and particularly for not letting the side down. He was a man of honour and known for it.

There are many who might say that a beating like that at school means nothing. They do not know, of course, that such beatings are discussed endlessly and the marks examined; they have no idea that in some cases the memory lingers on for many years and has its effect for life. No-one can say whether that episode, as dramatic in school terms as a hanging in a prison, affected Ward for the rest of his life or not. It surely made him keep silent when he could so easily have opened his mouth and told all.

Whatever the experts may think, Ward's sexual tastes, which developed rapidly once he was free of the parsonage, were not those of a normal young man. He liked the perverted, and although he indulged in the normal act, it was watching that turned him on. As the years went on many things aroused him: watching men and women perform, watching or indulging in group sex, making love to girls in high heels and silk stockings and becoming excited by flagellation. He shocked people by describing what he liked and by providing them with the chance to see what he liked, whether at his own or other people's parties. It may all have been perverse but those who took part did it because they too liked it and enjoyed it. For many years this was Ward's life. His final degradation can probably be compared to that of a drug addict: in the end he had to try something different, something stronger, with more kick, to give him the excitement and experience that was once gained from more normal sex.

It is interesting to note that when Ward began to sink to the depths, he was for a time a tenant of the flat once occupied by both Denis Hamilton, one-time husband of the British cinema sex-symbol Diana Dors, and Peter Rachman, a former Pole whose actions as a slum landlord in London and his means of getting rid of tenants he did not want – dogs, heavy gangs, over-crowding, violence and harassment – were so infamous that his name became a word in the language. All three, Ward, Hamilton and Rachman, had one thing in common: a love for sex and for discussing the highs and lows of their actions. Hamilton was a specialist in two-way mirrors and had one in the flat so that he could watch, with other guests, couples performing. Rachman enjoyed sex and for a time Christine Keeler and her teenage friend Mandy Rice-Davies were his mistresses. He was a generous and witty man, belying his appalling professional life and his odd sexual habits, which included walking in, stripping and having his current mistress straddle him with her bottom to his face so she never saw his reaction.

However, when Lewis and his wife were first on the fringe of his set, Ward was an urbane man on the way up. After leaving home he had visited France, Hamburg and London, and had spent five years in Kirksville, Missouri, getting his degree in osteopathy. He became Dr Ward shortly before the Second World War. He had been an officer at the end of the war and had been posted to India. It was the perfect place for a man of Ward's intelligence, smooth tongue and charm. An English officer who could play bridge, seduce the women with his silken voice, ease away the aches and pains of the Maharajahs with his fingers and sketch them as well was a treasure in Poona.

He did not settle easily in London after the war but his luck changed on the day the American ambassador, Averell Harriman, needed treatment. The American Embassy rang the clinic where Ward was working, asking for the name of an osteopath who could treat him. Ward thought for a moment and then rang back to recommend himself. It was a clever thing to do, and it was his opening to the world in which he longed to be.

For Ward was a snob and there was nothing he liked better apart from sex – and somehow he managed to keep the two worlds apart – than to mix with the royals who were his patients; they were also the subjects of his pen in a series of drawings he did for the *Illustrated London News*. Ward was a good artist and was commissioned by the *Daily Telegraph* to sketch scenes at the trial of Eichmann, the Nazi mass murderer.

Ward not only loved royalty but he enjoyed mixing with anyone who was famous: he was a champion name dropper. He just could not help it. He did have some famous names to drop in his great days, including those of Winston Churchill and several of his family, all patients or sitters for his portraits. He also painted his then bachelor friend Prince Philip, show business personalities such as Danny Kaye, Elizabeth Taylor and Frank Sinatra, and other famous people, including Paul Getty, Ward's great friend Lord 'Bill' Astor, and the former King of Yugoslavia.

Ward's social circle was large and interesting and his parties were a must for anyone who was someone and wanted fun. They were always bottle parties, because although Ward was a generous man when it came to spending time or sharing confidences with friends or opening up his flat for visitors, he was very tight usually when it came to spending money on them. Guests could stay as long as they liked but they had to pay for the food, drink and laundry. No-one was really sure whether he was desperately mean or just careless and unable to manage money. In his strange way it was probably the latter. He always had in his pocket cheques that he had not cashed or put into the bank. Although he lived a very high life he never spent much on himself, particularly when it came to clothes, just one decent suit and a sports jacket and flannels. He had sports cars, but they were always on hire purchase. He used his bridge club in Edgware Road as a place to cash cheques should he need ready money.

When Lewis first began really to know him, Ward had just married for the only time; the marriage lasted six weeks. He and the girl, a 21-year-old actress over ten years younger than he, knew by then that they could never get on. She sued him for divorce three years later, the year when Lewis fell out with him.

But to begin with, the Lewises found that Ward was fun, the

Mullallys and others in the crowd were fun and their social life was bustling. The Lewis marriage was not happy however. They had a daughter but Joy and her husband did not get on well and there were many rows. On occasions Joy would walk out of the flat in St John's Wood and roam the streets for a while as the heat of the row eased. By the early summer of 1952 the state of the marriage was such that she detested her husband. After one almighty row she walked out in tears and went to the place where she knew she would find sympathy and a shoulder on which to put her head while she told everything: Dr Ward's home in Devonshire Square.

Ward made her coffee and they sat while she talked and he listened. She told him about Lewis, what a pig he was, what he made her do sexually, what his attitude towards her was, how he did not think she lived up to what he expected of a wife and a hostess. Ward went on listening and there is no doubt that she talked well into the night and then went to bed. Ward went to his bed and nothing untoward happened.

It was a classic encounter: the lonely young wife, used to having her own way, in battle with a husband older than herself and equally used to having his own way but, because he was older, more experienced in the art of sticking to his guns. When the going got too bad she ran to find a comforter, someone who would listen to what she had to say and not scold her, criticize her. It happens all the time and there is no reason why the average husband should automatically suspect that the man to whom his wife turns for comfort should inevitably take her to bed.

Lewis was not an average husband. When she returned he questioned her hard for he was a bully who needed to dominate and humiliate verbally. He kept on and on at her until she told him where she had been and why and for how long. She said that Ward had been kind and listened to her which was more than *he* was doing.

That was it and nothing more.

Lewis did not believe her. He could not accept that his wife had spent the night at the flat of an attractive bachelor and not succumbed to his charms. And how could Ward spend the night with a girl as beautiful as his wife, for she was indeed beautiful, and not lay a finger on her?

Freddy Mullally explained it. He told me: 'Lewis was the

most suspicious husband in London. He never doubted that she had slept with Stephen because he could not imagine it possible for a man and a woman to be in a flat together throughout the night without having sex.' This was the single event that caused Lewis to hate Ward and swear vengeance. There was nothing more to it than that, and everything else followed from it. Mullally said: 'That was how the great obsession and hatred for Ward began. It never weakened, never faltered. It was intense, unremitting and skilfully designed to achieve its end. From there on he would pursue Ward right to the grave, whatever the cost.'

He went on to explain: 'The Profumo case would never have happened without John Lewis. It was his hatred for Stephen that started it. He never anticipated the actual outcome of course. No one could have but he started the ball rolling and kept it going and his hatred eventually got out of hand.'

Freddy's certainty is shared by many others who knew Lewis at the time and over the years that followed, as he worked to destroy Ward and made no bones about it to anyone who would listen.

Freddy summed it up thus: 'He was the sort of man who would wake up thinking: What can I do to get him today?'

5

THE MULLALLY LIBEL CASE

Each day Lewis woke up thinking of what he could do to harm Ward for the insult to his manhood. One friend said: 'He was a man who was acutely jealous of his wife even though his own behaviour was disgraceful. There is no stronger emotion in the world than sexual jealousy. In his case it ate into him like a worm in an apple.'

After he decided that Joy had been unfaithful he first threatened suicide and then told everyone about it. He shouted it loud and clear in the watering and eating holes of London and he went on so much that Ward took legal advice. As he raged, Lewis sucked in others such as Mullally.

He said: 'Shortly after this Joy left him. We used to go out as a four and have some good times, but the time came when she could no longer endure his behaviour to her as a husband.'

It was a strange situation. She could not bear to have him touch her and he made her flesh creep. She was in such a state that she went to her GP, a small man who listened to her tale of woe and came up with the fascinating and astonishing suggestion, for those days, that she should take a lover. The little doctor, who barely came up to her chest, was one of those whom Lewis put on his original list of co-respondents.

But just as Joy was about to pack and go, Lewis had a minor heart attack. He was seriously ill and was never to recover fully. Because he was so ill, Joy did not go but stayed on to see him through his illness. When he returned home her hatred had not abated but she stayed for three days as a dutiful wife. Then she went, taking their daughter with her in July 1952.

Her quick-tempered husband reacted with fury. He immediately filed for divorce and accused Mullally of

committing adultery with Joy five days before she had left him.
To this day, both of them deny absolutely that this happened.
They did so throughout the divorce that was so viciously fought,
and they do now.

But Lewis was out for blood. As soon as Joy had left he rang
Freddy, who describes the conversation:

> He insisted on the phone that I should come straight around
> although I said I was busy. He was in bed and he asked me if I
> had slept with Joy and I said of course I had not, which was true.
> Then he said 'You are either for me or against me,' and he
> demanded that my then wife, who was great friends with Joy,
> should spy on Joy because they were going to get a divorce. I
> said, 'Goodbye, I'm not getting my wife to spy for you', and that
> was it. That was why I, like Stephen, came under the hammer.
> From then on he worked like a demon to fake evidence against
> us. He hired private detectives and even tried to persuade the
> *Daily Express* that Stephen and I were running a call-girl racket.

Lewis had already anonymously rung West End Central police
station to tell them the same story but it got him nowhere. The
Inland Revenue also received calls and anonymous letters about
Ward, suggesting that he was not declaring what he had earned
and would be worth investigating. They did this, but never
turned up any wrong-doing, just that his poor accounting meant
he owed back tax. When Lewis rang a friend on the *Express*
about the call-girls, he assumed they would act and they did.

Freddy, who was then married to Suzanne Warner, formerly
Howard Hughes's publicity representative in Europe, was rung
one morning by an agitated Ward. He had had a reporter from
the *Express* around, telling him that they had been 'tipped off'
(but not saying by whom) and they wanted to know what Ward
had to say about this racket.

Freddy was a former assistant editor of *Tribune*, the Socialist
paper, and political editor of the Sunday Pictorial. He had
contacts in the Labour government at the highest level and knew
the newspaper world well. He rang his friend Arthur
Christiansen, the editor of the *Express*, made an appointment
and went round to tell him what was going on.

Christiansen, the architect of the *Express* success story under
Lord Beaverbrook, (it sold over four million a day then), called

in his news editor, Morley Richards, and asked where the tip had come from. Morley, like the great news editor he was, hummed and shifted ground in his determination not to reveal his source, but when Freddy mentioned the name of Lewis it was obvious that it was he who had given the tip. Christiansen declared that would be the end of it and Mullally and Ward would not be troubled again.

Freddy told Ward what he had done and suggested he should not bother to sue Lewis for slander. It was enough that his pathetic effort had been frustrated.

It was best to leave it. Lewis was livid and rang the police again, anonymously, to insist that Ward was procuring girls for his wealthy patients.

Let us consider Lewis as he was at this moment in 1952. He had lost his seat in the House and because he was suspected, with considerable justificiation, of using inside knowledge to boost his fortune by manipulating his shares before a big deal with the Coal Board, there was little likelihood of his getting another seat. But his business was flourishing. He owned horses which ran well and he made money with his gambling. His marriage was over, but that did not stop him getting women the way he always had – by paying them. He had no skill in chit-chat with women. Paying them to do what he wanted was a much easier and quicker way of satisfying his lust. He was known by the girls in the night-clubs as the man with the largest number of hands. His skill in fumbling and groping was formidable.

He was tolerated on the fringe of the crowd with whom he used to run nightly and he was as familiar in the restaurants and bars of the West End as he was at race meetings. He took part in some good pranks with his friends, for he could turn on the charm when needed; he paid his corner and was known as a generous host. He liked to show off his wealth. He had some valuable paintings on the walls of his flat, including a Goya, and a safe which was always packed with cash. The flat was opulently furnished with reproduction Chippendale and other pieces and he gave parties which included film stars as guests. He lent his flat to Ava Gardner for a while and had an unrequited passion for the Irish film star Kathleen Ryan, who had starred in *Odd Man Out*.

Freddy Mullally knew him well, first as a friend and then as a bitter enemy. His views are those of others who knew Lewis.

They all agreed that he was not a nice man but could be charming when he wanted something. Freddy described him as follows:

He was a snappy dresser, very Jewish, brought up a spoilt young man, the eldest in the family. He was arrogant and he looked it because he walked in a truculent sort of way with his nose up in the air. But on first meeting, if he needed something from you, he was charming. Most people came to dislike him although they were happy at first to take his drinks. Poor Dominic Elwes who later committed suicide was a superb mimic and he took John off so well and amusingly. He had John to a 'T'.

Lewis could be absurdly pompous and sycophantic to the front bench and the Labour party leaders. But the shrewder of them were aware of his weaknesses: women, drinking, gambling, slight dodginess in business and a potential threat to the party.

He thought money could get him everything and he was not above bribery.

He even tried it at the Board of Trade and it became so serious, according to Tom Driberg, that Harold Wilson, who was then in charge, had him banned from the building. He made a lot of money at the race meetings doing the same kind of thing. He and his friends discussed what was what before a meeting and would decide on the winner in certain small races. He was well informed about horses and owned some good ones in his time.

All his friends knew about his sex life. Freddy said:

He had girl-friends. He had a girl in a flat in Shepherd's Bush and he once took me round there to show her off and tell me that she would give me the works if I ever needed it.

He never had success with straight girls although he tried hard. The trouble was that he was a 'slam, bang thank-you-mam' operator. The only women who seemed to turn him on, apart from his wife, were whores because they were easy. He did not have to court them or be nice to them, just pay them.

He had a problem in that he saw everyone as a potential enemy. He was insecure. He had been a successful MP with a good business and a beautiful wife. When he married Joy she was a Jewish princess and it was a marriage with great potential. But as things went wrong perhaps he thought everything he had was being eroded.

Freddy and Ward's crowd knew one thing for certain: Lewis was a man who knew how to hate. Freddy said:

> When he hated his face screamed the fact. His eyes would narrow as he talked of those who had crossed him. He would grind his teeth and spit out the words. It was total malice. He would say 'I'll get him, whatever it costs.' And he wasn't putting on an act. He meant it.

Freddy was the pig in the middle when it came to the divorce. He was heavily involved in the break-up of the marriage and in what happened between Ward and Joy Lewis. He said:

> Lewis was a chauvinist and a bully. When he married Joy there was a lot of money in prospect. She was a great catch, reputedly the most beautiful wife of any MP at the time.
>
> They used to fight and occasionally she would walk out. She had no one to turn to. They were friendly with Stephen Ward, the attraction for Lewis being that Stephen and his crowd always had a lot of pretty girls in tow.
>
> I liked Stephen. You never saw him depressed. He was always vivacious and sparkling with good humour and bonhomie and always at the disposal of a friend in trouble or who needed a bed. Joy and he talked through the night but nothing happened. They never had an affair, ever, but it was the first time that she had stayed out all night and Lewis could never give her the benefit of the doubt.

Freddy remembers what happened next because it cost him thousands:

> He had an obsessive need to win his divorce action and was prepared to spend a fortune on it. He bribed people right and left to get them to provide evidence, true or false. Here's an example: he paid a man at a Berkeley Square garage to say that he called at my flat and Joy answered the door in her nightdress. It was rubbish, totally untrue. But everything was grist to the mill. In fact, he originally cited as a co-respondent practically any male who had crossed the threshold of his flat in the recent past. Finally the list was reduced to one co-respondent – me. He had let Stephen off in a deal over slander. Stephen said he would not sue if Lewis left him out of the divorce. Lewis had no choice.

Freddy continued:

> When the divorce finally came to court two years later it was one of the most bitterly fought and expensive of any such cases. Lewis wanted to make a big splash and he did, having spent the two years collecting his 'evidence'. And the judge bought it all, refusing to give credit to anything said on behalf of Joy or myself. Lewis hadn't wasted his time or his money.
>
> He got me first and cleaned me out. That left Stephen, and that took much longer.

The divorce was the second time Lewis had struck at Mullally through the courts. Earlier, he had pounced when Mullally, as he says now, did a naive thing for an experienced journalist: he put an apology in writing. When Lewis got to hear of it he almost ruined him over it.

Some time after the Lewises had split, Mullally heard that Lewis had paid someone £100 in notes (from the safe he kept behind a painting in his lounge in Abbey Lodge) to obtain evidence for the divorce. The alleged recipient was Dennis Kennerley Edwards, a former employee in a publicity organization set up by Mullally. There was some dispute as to what was said when the two men met in September 1952 in Mayfair's Fine Arts Club but a few days later Mullally wrote a letter to Edward's solicitor saying it had been a case of mistaken identity. He also enclosed an apology to three other journalists who had been present.

When Lewis heard about it, saw the letters and spoke to Edwards, he moved as swiftly as a rat down a sewer. He issued a writ and a year before the divorce there was an expensive and high-powered warm-up in the High Court. The loser would have to pay the bill and it was going to be a large one.

The hearing started on 30 November 1953, the year of the Coronation of Elizabeth II, in front of Mr Justice Hilberry and a jury. Gilbert Paull, QC, and Bernard Gillis appeared for Lewis, and Derek Curtis-Bennett, QC, and T. Springer for Mullally.

Lewis claimed that Mullally slandered him by imputing that he paid Edward £100 to give information which would be useful in Lewis's divorce. Lewis also sued for libel on the grounds that when Mullally wrote the letter to Edwards' solicitor and the three journalists, withdrawing the allegation against Edwards, he inferred that Lewis had paid the money to someone else.

Mullally said that the words were not defamatory, refused to admit he had published the alleged slander, and pleaded privilege. Lewis retaliated by saying that if the occasion was privileged, then Mullally was actuated by malice.

In his full statement of claim, which was read to the jury, Lewis said that two months after he had cited Mullally as co-respondent in his divorce, Mullally met Edwards in the Fine Arts Club on 30 September 1952 and said to him: 'I do not wish to speak to you as I have read in an affidavit that you have accepted £100 from John Lewis to provide information about me.'

A few days later Mullally, he claimed, wrote a letter to Edwards' solicitor, saying:

> I am satisfied that the description given by an eye-witness of the person who received a sum of £100 from John Lewis might well have fitted someone else. Your client will probably believe me when I say that I am more than happy to learn that, since it seemed to me incredible that a person of your client's character – not to mention his past friendship with me – should accept such a commission.

The letter went on to withdraw the allegation. The copy letter to the other journalists said: 'Further enquiries which I have made convince me that a certain eye-witness's description of the action which I attributed to Kennerley was in fact a description of somebody else and someboy else's action.'

Mullally cannot even now explain what made him write the letter. He knew he should not put anything like that in writing, even if it was true. It was like water to a man dying of thirst to Lewis, who was looking for any way 'to get' Mullally.

Lewis made no bones about what he considered the words meant when he put his statement before the jury. He said they implied that he was prepared to pay for false evidence and that he was unfit to hold public or political office. Mullally said they meant nothing of the sort. It took three expensive days to sort it out.

Paull, QC, opened the case to the jury by saying that the letter and words might be a deliberate attempt to blacken Lewis's character for an ulterior motive. Lewis was a man of some public character, he said, and it was soon after Lewis married in February 1948 that he came to know Mullally; the Lewises and Mullallys were on visiting terms. On 28 June 1952 Lewis had his coronary and after Joy had left he cited Mullally as co-respondent. On 14 November he received a written denial. The divorce action had not yet come to court.

Edwards, said Paull, had been employed by Mullally for about a year. Paull then told how the two had met in the Fine Arts Club and what Edwards claimed was said and about the letters.

Paull said that under the guise of withdrawing the allegations against Edwards, Mullally was making an attack on Lewis. Edwards insisted there was no truth in the matter. His solicitors had been careful to put the exact words he alleged Mullally had spoken and Mullally did not deny at the time that he had in fact said them. But four months later he amended his defence to say that he had not spoken the words as cited.

Edwards repeated everything from the witness box. He said that although Mullally had sacked him, there was no animosity between them. He also said that the words set out in the allegation of slander and no others, were the words used.

Lewis was his usual confident self, giving his evidence convincingly without being shaken. He said that there was not the slightest truth in the suggestion that he had been paying people to give information in the way alleged.

Curtis-Bennett wanted to know where the imputation was against Lewis's character. Lewis made it plain: 'If, in fact, it is suggested that someone pays someone else £100 to give evidence in a case where they may be under oath in the witness box the inference to be drawn is that it is false evidence.'

Had he been making inquiries to back up his divorce petition? 'Certain people came to me who were horrified with my wife's cruelty and gave me evidence upon which the petition was served.' And yes, he had employed inquiry agents and later two more names were added as co-respondents. However, he had not paid a tall man with a moustache (and Edwards had a distinctive moustache) £50 or £100.

Curtis-Bennett continued questioning: 'You are riddled with spite against Mr Mullally?'

'I certainly have no love for him,' Lewis said, which with hindsight can be regarded as an understatement.

'He happens to deny this adultery.'

'He will have plenty of chance to defend himself,' Lewis retorted.

'Meanwhile you hate him, do you not?' It was a fair question. Lewis gave a fair answer which, again with hindsight, was exactly what one would expect him to give. He was saying what he genuinely believed and would not accept that it might not be so. He said:

'I have seen the evidence against Mr Mullally and I am wholly satisfied in my own mind that he had committed adultery with my wife.'

Curtis-Bennett then turned to the accusation that the slander and libel Lewis claimed implied he was unfit for political office. Lewis said he had hopes of becoming a member of parliament again. He agreed, however, that the Labour party had refused to endorse his nomination as a candidate; but this had nothing to do with his moral character. He was 'not in the slightest' ashamed of anything he had done.

When Curtis-Bennett opened the case for Mullally he said that the words complained of were not in law capable of a defamatory meaning and the words spoken in the club and the letters, were used on occasions of qualified privilege.

But the judge was against him. He said the words were in law capable of a defamatory meaning, that the occasion was not privileged but the letters were clearly of qualified privilege. What the jury would have to decide was whether, in both cases, they were actuated by malice.

Mullally said in evidence that once Lewis and Joy had parted he saw nothing more of Lewis but he and his wife had seen Joy. He had seen her only in his wife's company or with friends. He said the allegations of adultery were untrue.

The judge intervened. 'I am not going to allow a discussion on the truth or otherwise of matters in the divorce case.'

So Mullally stuck to his meeting with Edwards. He said that he told him: 'I will have a drink with you, Kennerley, when you have proved to me that you have returned the £100 John Lewis gave you for getting information about me.' (Mullally had been told that a man with a big moustache had been paid £100 in notes out of Lewis's stacked wall safe to get some dirt on Mullally. He had got the wrong man when he thought it was Edwards.)

Edwards, Mullally went on, said: 'You have got it all wrong' – or something similar. Curtis-Bennett asked him: 'Were you actuated by any malice towards Mr Lewis?'

'No, I have no malice towards anyone, even in spite of what has happened. Malice is not part of my equipment.' Mullally said that his letters were concerned only with his position with Edwards. He said it was not true that he was intending 'to make it worse' for Lewis.

Paull, QC, put it to him in stronger terms: 'From the moment the divorce petition was served did you make up your mind to do Mr Lewis as much harm as possible?'

'Certainly not,' said Mullally, maintaining that it was absolute nonsense to say that in the letters he was trying to implicate Lewis.

Both sides threw some dirt in their closing speeches. Curtis-Bennett said that the words and letters could not possibly be construed in the way Lewis claimed. The jury might well think that in view of his pending divorce, Lewis was more likely to be malicious than Mullally. Lewis had shown his malice towards Mullally in the witness box and by almost every word that he spoke.

'He spat out his words at Mullally,' Curtis-Bennett contended and added: 'You may think this is an attempt to win a battle before the real battle comes on in another court.'

Paull gave exactly the opposite interpretation. He said: 'When all sorts of accusations are made, without any foundation of fact whatsoever, against a man in the witness box, I venture to say it is the duty of the jury to make quite certain that he walks out of this court without people saying, "Well, there might have been something in it after all." Malice screams from Mr Mullally.'

The judge summed up briefly, explaining to the jury the legal definitions of malice and privilege. Malice, he said was not confined in meaning to mere personal spite. It was stronger than that, and if Mullally had used an occasion of privilege – meaning when he wrote the letter – when motivated by malice, it was an improper use. Mullally had, of course, denied that this was ever his intention. The judge, however, pointed out that Mullally from first to last had never put on record any statement that what he had said was true.

The judge also told the jury that if they found that Mullally had been moved by malice, then they should award damages but should use their common sense when fixing them. They should remember, he said, that the money was coming out of someone else's pocket. If they wanted to be generous they should do so when the money came out of their own pockets.

The jury was out for two hours and then came back to ask the judge for further directions on the exact meaning of malice and for some direction as to the classification of damages. They came back again an hour later. They had decided that what Mullally said to Edwards in the Fine Arts Club implied that Lewis had committed a criminal offence, that the letters sent to the solicitor were defamatory of Lewis and, worse, that they were activated by malice. This meant a total of £700 damages and, on top of that, around £1,500 costs. Mullally's heart sank.

The case rambled on into a third day with legal arguments which gave the judge the chance to say: 'Having regard to the way in which the case was conducted I should have thought that £700 was not a penny too much in the way of damages. It seems to me a very sensible sum.'

Not to Mullally. He said recently: 'Lewis was a vindictive bastard. If someone crossed him it became an obsession for him to get him. He said he would get Stephen and me over Joy, whatever happened. He got me with the libel and the divorce. He got his costs and cleaned me out.

'That left Stephen.'

It was to take Lewis eleven years.

6

DIVORCE

There is no better public clue to Lewis's obsession and hatred once he had been hurt – or thought he had been – than his divorce action against Joy, which she fought with equal hatred and loathing. It lasted for fourteen days during the end of November and the beginning of December, 1954. The judge, Mr Justice Sachs, said at the end of it that the trial had been fought with a consistent and virulent bitterness which could have rarely been exceeded, and neither party had spared either pain or expense in the fight. He added that the conflict of evidence had been so acute that he wished there had been a jury to decide the issues.

Divorce was quite a different procedure in those days. There were no quickies, no waiting a couple of years before nipping down to the court to end a marriage that had started on such a high note and had ended flatter than last year's champagne. To obtain an ordinary divorce on a complaint of adultery, whether trumped up or not, was a complicated, difficult and embarrassing affair. Even if you and your spouse had been unhappy, had found different partners and agreed to split, you could not simply file for divorce and start again just like that.

It involved a detailed plan of action so hypocritical and silly that the French in particular laughed openly at the antics of the British. The usual method was for the husband to go to an agency which specialized in providing partners for a dirty night away, so that adultery could be established. Sex did not come into it. The husband and his partner went to a hotel and booked in under some clever name such as Smith. They spent the evening having a drink and a meal, and then went to the bedroom but not the bed together. A private detective employed by the wife was often on the scene to observe what was afoot and he would take notes, ready for his sworn statement to the judge. A cheaper idea was not to have a detective on the spot, but to arrange for him later to interview the chambermaid who brought the morning tea and found – surprise, surprise – the husband sitting up with his partner in bed. The detective would see the chambermaid afterwards and at a later date would give his evidence before the judge.

The husband would make a statement admitting adultery with the hired girl, although in some cases the wife might be cross enough to accuse her husband of adultery with his real girl-friend and name her, when the husband would reluctantly agree. The judge would grant a decree nisi. It was essential that once this had happened neither party should have sex with the person they now loved and wanted to marry because this might come to the ear (or eye) of authorities such as the Queen's Proctor. This would stop the absolution of the decree nisi which came some months later.

If the parties contested each other's accusations, particularly when it came to cruelty in addition to adultery or unreasonable behaviour, and had the money to do so, the case would end up with much legal representation before a High Court red judge in the Probate, Divorce and Admiralty Division.

A great deal of mud was thrown, cruel, vicious mud. No holds were barred, nothing was held back, no accusation, however old, wounding or out of context, was left out as the pent-up hatreds and loathings of the years came spewing out. All this was possible because the press were not allowed to report what was said by the witnesses. But they were able to print every word the judge said in his judgment; and there were judges who seemed to enjoy relating in detail the evidence they had heard, all of which was taken down by the press and passed on to the public, who loved it.

Thus, at the end of the Lewis v Lewis divorce, the judge told all. It is not so much the detail, fascinating as it is, that is important. What is of more interest is the behaviour of Lewis and the way in which he pinpointed and made a target of those he hated.

The parties assembled in the Strand and went into the cavernous court where events that had stirred so much passion and hatred were now recounted in the sombre and stiff surroundings of the legal theatre.

To help sort out the accounts on both sides, which clashed

dramatically in every detail, leading lights of the legal world assembled at great expense. Gilbert Paull, QC, aided by John Latey, appeared for Lewis. Paull, as a judge, was later to try an action in which Lewis was the plaintiff. Mrs Lewis had Gilbert Beyfus, QC, the 'Grey Fox' and the darling of the press, the barrister rich and top people plumped for when in trouble. Freddy Mullally, who had good reason after his losing action the year before to expect that he would be under tremendous pressure, was represented by Colin Sleeman.

For fourteen days the couple and their witnesses, a total of twenty-nine, spat out their hate, venom, loathing and malice, and hurled their insults. But exactly what was said has gone for ever, because there is no 30 Year Rule under which such words become public property. But the gist – and a lively gist it was – is available because the judge, in his discretion, was able to give the public a rich helping of the facts. He was scathing (and almost vicious about some of the witnesses) as he gave his judgment at the end of the case, which cost £15,000 (the equivalent of over £120,000 in today's money).

The bare allegations he had to consider were these:

Lewis claimed that his wife Joy had committed adultery with Mullally, which both of them denied, and with two other men who were later dismissed from the case; and he also alleged cruelty. He complained of Joy's attitude towards his family and the entertainment of his political and business friends. He went further. He claimed that she sometimes struck him or kicked out and that her treatment of him after his illness was cruel.

Joy, in return, claimed that Lewis had sex with a woman named only as NJT and with another woman, and that he too was cruel. She said that he frequently visited prostitutes at their homes and two witnesses had been with him on these expeditions. Lewis strongly denied this and accused the witnesses of conspiracy to falsify the evidence. Joy also said that throughout their marriage her husband had a violent temper and was a man of domineering arrogance who humiliated, slapped and assaulted her. In July 1952 she suffered from ranting, screaming abuse, insults and false accusations (as on the night she wept on Ward's shoulder) and was finally ousted from her rightful control of the house. She also said she suffered from her husband's drunkenness.

Lewis, said the judge, was an intelligent man with a quick

mind. He had his fair share of charm in personal relationships but had a quick temper. He liked his own way and was apt to become unduly excited when crossed and could be overbearing at times. He said that Lewis had plainly become embittered towards his wife during the events that led to the break-up of the marriage. He had developed suspicions and antagonisms which had warped his views and to some extent his memory. This had led him in some instances to make accusations for which there was no foundation and which ought never to have never been made the subject of a charge of cruelty, and indeed, some of his evidence about Joy did not ring true.

Mr Justice Sachs said that the couple had married in 1948, Joy being sixteen years younger than her husband, and they had a daughter in 1950. The marriage continued on its far from happy way until July 1952, when Lewis had a heart attack; three days after he had been discharged from hospital Joy left home. A fortnight later Lewis filed a petition for divorce with his charge of adultery.

Joy, the judge said, was a young woman 'of graceful and well-dressed aspect', and came from 'a well-circumstanced home'. By 1949 she began to dislike her husband and by 1952 that 'graduated to hate'. Her powers of detestation were well proved by the evidence. If anyone opposed her, he declared, there were few limits to which she would not go, and she was not hampered by scruples.

She was educated at a well-known school and had now come into her share of the family fortune. Her ability to charm when she chose was unchallengeable and she was of a type exceptionally attractive to many men. She had impressed the judge because her intelligence and poise had not deserted her during cross-examination, and rarely did she lose the half smile on her face. But her manner to her husband had been described by witnesses as cold and hard, completely heartless, very callous and terribly cruel. During their marriage she wrote spiteful entries in her diary about her husband and left them about so the servants could read them.

The judge said: 'She was never really in love with her husband though it is not clear whether one of her motives for marrying him – as was said by counsel – was to escape from her home.' He accepted Lewis's evidence that if she was not getting her way in an argument she would say: 'If you do not do what I

want I will scream,' and on occasions did so. The judge declared
that he was forced to the unhappy but clear conclusion that her
evidence could not be relied upon as establishing any fact which
was neither an admission nor a fact fully corroborated by a
reliable witness.

Ward was not a witness at all. A deal had been done to keep
his strong evidence out. Lewis had been shouting from the
rooftops that Ward had obtained Joy for Mullally, and Ward –
• understandably, because it was quite untrue, as was the adultery
charge – was in the process of issuing a writ for slander. Ward
was happy to tell all he knew for Joy's sake, but in the end was
kept out because Lewis agreed not to name Ward if Ward
withdrew any action for slander. He did. There was also a
feeling that Ward's evidence might cause more trouble than it
was worth.

The judge turned back to Lewis who, he said, had hoped for a
bride who would grace the life of a public man. He was
disappointed and from the witness box said so: 'Actors and
models – those were the sort of people who were brought to my
house' (although later he was happy to host parties given to such
people). The judge referred to Lewis's public life too, as MP, as
parliamentary private secretary to the Postmaster-General, and
to his activities with the British Boxing Board of Control.

That the judge was on Lewis's side became clear when he
started to give his views on the witnesses and their evidence for
Joy. He did not mince words or refrain from scathing comment,
and was biting in his verdicts and opinions. First he tore apart
the Mullallys. Freddy, as we know, was a distinguished
journalist and publicist. His wife, a close friend of Joy's was
public relations officer in England to multi-millionaire film
producer Howard Hughes. The judge said that the Mullallys
were 'the focal point for some celebrities and their glamour
which Mrs Lewis might have thought epitomized a gay life'.
Mullally, the judge said, and one can almost hear the sneer in
his tone, was a well turned-out young man who recited parts of
his evidence in a mechanical way, possibly because he came
from a police family. It was clear – and it often showed in his
face – that Mullally had a deep seated malice against Lewis. He
recalled the jury verdict the year before that Mullally was
actuated by express malice in publishing a libel against Lewis.
Mrs Mullally, the judge considered, was 'smart, well-dressed

and with a power of charm parallel in many ways to that of her friend, Mrs Lewis'.

The judge mentioned part of Mullally's evidence which concerned Jeanne M ..., a seventeen-year old actress who was later to win international fame. She was called to give evidence about an alleged admission by Mullally of misconduct with Joy. Miss M said she was lured by a false story to visit Mullally at a flat in Dolphin Square one Sunday, where she expected to meet someone who would help her further her career. Instead, she claimed that Mullally made improper advances to her while they were alone in the flat and spoke to her about what he had been doing with Joy – something like 'a romp' with her, although the judge, who believed her, did not rely on her precise memory of the words. Mullally denied it.

Mullally said, the judge continued, that it was not a fixed meeting, that he had borrowed the key while in the company of others in case the girl wanted to set up home there, and he had not made an advance. However, Mullally said that Lewis had been with them too and it was he who made an advance. Mullally suggested that the girl had told her story because she was actuated by spite as he had failed to advance her career.

The judge said he accepted the girl's word and then firmly destroyed the Mullallys' case. 'Their evidence must be wholly ruled out,' was the verdict judicial.

Nearly forty years on, Freddy Mullally says: 'He was biased against us from the start and he made no bones about it. He would routinely make a point of bowing when he came into court and Lewis bowed back. From the start of the case he treated the distinguished Gilbert Beyfus, who was acting for Joy, with outright hostility.'

The judge turned to 'Y', once named as a co-respondent. Mr Justice Sachs said that 'Y' had the merit of neither professing any undue education nor putting on airs. Despite his financial success, his moral outlook was not on a par, for he regarded his blatant misconduct with a common prostitute as quite normal behaviour and thought any other views were prudish. Thus, the judge declared to no-one's surprise, 'Y's standard of reliability fell far short of what was required and 'would not be acted upon. I have little doubt that much of it was malicious invention.'

So much for Mr 'Y'! Next to feel the sharp edge of the acid tongue was the doctor in the case, who had been the family doctor for the Lewis family for twenty-five years. He had a practice in west London and his evidence was considered by Beyfus as being odd and reprehensible and by Paull as quite abhorrent.

The doctor had said that in 1949 he found that Lewis had become 'sexually repulsive' to his wife.

The judge went on: 'The doctor said he had never found a case where the repugnance of the wife was so great. In 1951 he advised the wife in these striking words: 'Find yourself a lover.' In his evidence he made it quite clear that he meant her to find a man with whom to commit misconduct. I find that advice was given seriously and indeed the doctor was at some pains to make it plain that the course he took was correct and that he regarded the wife as fertile receipt of such advice.'

It was not a question of bias. The doctor claimed he loved Lewis like a son but the judge thought that unconsciously he had been indoctrinated by Joy 'in visits to a young woman of charm'.

The judge accepted some of the doctor's evidence and did not think his advice was the cause of the break-up of the marriage. He said: 'The basic trouble that in due course broke up the marriage was the clash of personality.'

Having disposed of the main witnesses, the judge considered the allegations about Lewis's adultery with the unknown women. He dismissed them because they relied on worthless evidence given 'with a degree of venom and relish you could hardly fail to notice 'by Mullally amd Mr 'Y'. He then turned to the woman named by Joy as someone with whom her husband had committed adultery, known as N.J.T. or 'Jacky' of 'X' Gardens.

Mr 'Y' said he had been there and had watched Lewis 'committing misconduct' with Jacky. Lewis hotly denied this and furthermore he produced another man named John Lewis, a 'neat, clerkly little man' as a witness, who gave his name as John Henry Lewis. He said that he was at Jacky's flat when an agent for Joy arrived to ask questions.

Jacky asked what John was doing, involving her in a divorce case and this John Lewis said he was doing nothing of the sort; it was absolutely ridiculous because his wife did not want a divorce.

When the agent asked further questions, Jacky said that the

man with her was the only John Lewis she knew and the judge accepted that the man he saw in the witness box was telling the truth. He totally rejected Mr 'Y's' evidence.

Then the judge moved on to his decision. He said that the charges of cruelty that each brought against the other were a long way from being established, and much of Lewis's case on that point had very properly been abandoned. All of Joy's cruelty allegations failed completely. He preferred, on balance, Lewis's view of them. He referred to one of Lewis's charges, that at a reception his wife said that it was not for her to go and shake hands with a receiving ambassador, adding 'Let the ... ambassador come to me,': that was not cruelty. But, the judge said, he did not accept Joy's allegations of vile and abusive language and excessive drinking by her husband.

The judge also thought that when the doctor advised Joy to find herself a lover it was exactly the sort of advice that suited her. He accepted that since 1950 Joy had visited Mullally at his flat when his wife was not there. He then had another go at Mullally, saying that evidence had been given that his ambition was to sleep with all the beautiful women in London, including Joy. The judge ruled that adultery did take place at the flat in Hay Hill in July 1952, an allegation which both Mullally and Joy still deny absolutely.

The judge found that Joy had acted in a way that constituted cruelty when she left Lewis after his heart attack, taking their daughter with her. He said that by June 1952 Joy was planning to divorce her husband, but his illness interrupted her plans. At the outset she was shocked into acting as a dutiful wife, but hatred showed in the hard and cutting things she said. When she left him, Lewis was recovering from a coronary thrombosis: it was that action which constituted cruelty.

Joy's allegations of adultery by her husband completely failed. They depended on worthless evidence by two of her men witnesses. The red judge had one more dagger to stab in before his verdict. He said that the doctor's advice to Joy to take a lover, which, if his dates were right, served to confirm rather than instigate adultery by Joy, was not something on which he should comment, as it might come before a professional body.

All that remained was for the judge to grant Lewis a decree nisi on the grounds of adultery and cruelty by his wife; her answer that Lewis had committed adultery and been cruel so that she should be awarded the divorce, was dismissed. The judge ordered that Joy and Mullally should pay three-quarters of Lewis's costs and that Mullally should pay half of the sum; this meant he had to find £10,000, a crippling debt that hit him hard for some time.

Ward left the court with Joy's group. Lewis rejoiced that he had won, but seethed with loathing at the sight of Ward for whom he blamed the end of his marriage. He wanted to pay him back and he made no bones about the fact that he would not be satisfied until he had done so. Any fortune teller would have been laughed out of business if she had forecast what was going to happen in the next decade.

7

THE FIFTIES

After the divorce there was a lull in Lewis's life. 1954 was a
bitter year. In the March he had finally withdrawn his
nomination to re-contest Bolton West for the next election. It
was not really his choice. He was still keen to contest a seat he
was sure he could win, and his friends in the Lancashire town
knew he would do well because he was still popular, but those in
power in Labour headquarters blocked his nomination. His
divorce had not helped his cause, but that was after he had
withdrawn his nomination. There had been loud whispers about
the way he was proceeding, and the fact that he was chasing
witnesses. There was Lewis's persecution of Ward, his
incessant claims that he had slept with his wife and his threats
about what he was going to do to him. There was his case
against Freddy, and the fact that it had broken the journalist,
who was well liked by those who knew him in the Labour party.
People who had known the Lewises and the Mullallys as a
foursome found it difficult to understand the great, open hatred
Lewis had for Freddy, particularly after such a good friendship.
Most people did not believe that Freddy and Joy slept together.
Both denied it absolutely. People did not believe that Ward had
slept with her either. It was not his kind of behaviour at all, and
he denied it as vehemently as she did.

Lewis could be amusing and interesting when he chose,
which was often, but he spoilt it sometimes by his attitude
towards waiters. He was rude and arrogant and treated them as
if they were second-class citizens which embarrassed those who
were with him.

One of his friends, war hero and club owner Eddie Chapman,
said:

He could be fine, good company, a laugh. Once we had a great joke, two of us dressing up as Arabs to fool the guy who ran Les Ambassadeurs which was one of our favourite places. We were always there, the whole crowd, eating and drinking, and we all had a great deal of fun. John could have a lot of fun but he had this vengeful streak and when he had that he was awful.

Anyway, two of us dressed as Arabs and John took us in his Roller down to Paddy Kennedy's pub, The Star in Belgravia, where everyone used to meet before we went off to eat and go clubbing. We took everyone in, no-one noticed who we were and we chatted away as if we were the real thing. We finally got into the Roller and John drove us down to Les Ambassadeurs and in we went and the owner, John Mills was completely taken in. John Lewis said we were very rich and he believed him and he was sweeping the floor in greeting. We were terrible. We sent everything back, all the food, all the drink, said it was bad or we weren't allowed to eat it and they kow-towed to us and did everything we said and changed it all. We were there a long time and John played his part very well indeed.

As we went out we said something in English so that the owner would know who we were and suddenly the secret was out and everyone had a good laugh, no-one minded, it was a good joke and that's how it was in those days. It wasn't the end of it. We went to the Churchill's and again John Lewis introduced us as rich Arab princes, over here on a visit. They gave us a table at the front for the cabaret and it wasn't very good, a couple of ballet dancers, and just as a ballerina was hoisted up we threw two fireworks which went off with a tremendous bang and the girl fell down on to her head. We Arabs pointed to two businessmen who were clearly there on a visit to London. They were picked up and run out of the club and thrown into the street. We had a great evening.

Others tell of how Lewis was usually on the fringe of the group, a chap who had difficulty in holding his drink and who threw good parties. He liked to manage the guests and was a bit pretentious when it came to treasures such as his paintings and chairs. He would also telephone his stockbroker so that everyone could hear.

Another acquaintance said;

Sometimes he was all right. But then he would switch and become pigheaded, arrogant and pompous, with no charm, no wit and certainly no compassion. He could be amusing and interesting and he could be a bore with a great ego, having to show off.

He was out of the action for a while in the late fifties when he was nabbed by a burglar. It was not funny for him but everyone else had a laugh because it was so ridiculous. He had come home when he was living alone after the divorce, and there was a burglar in his lovely flat.

As soon as John put the key in the lock, the burglar dived behind the door and hid. When John came in the burglar stepped forward and bit him hard on the nose, gripping it like a dog would. It was a very tight grip, really painful because as you know, being bitten on the nose is a very painful thing indeed. He hung on and then when John was screaming and writhing in agony he let go and ran out, leaving John with a very scarred and sore hooter. He had a big hooter being a Jewish boy and it left a terrible mark.

He went to the doctor and had it bandaged up but he was not able to go out for some weeks because it took a long time to heal. It was a shame, and they never did catch the burglar.

For the rest of the fifties Lewis played the field at the races, occasionally meeting up with George Wigg, an important contact for the future, had a good time with the girls, did well at business, had Gordon Richards, one of the finest jockeys of all time, to train his horses, and carried on suing. He had two big wins in High Court actions, both cases involving famous and expensive names in the legal world.

In 1958 Lewis was sued by a former Labour MP, Herschel Lewis Austin, and his company, which with Lewis's company, had a virtual monopoly of the rubber belting used in coal mines. The issue was whether Lewis had promised to pay a £5,000 commission to Austin for services in a take-over bid for another company. The promise, Austin claimed, was made during a conversation at Lewis's flat in July 1956. Lewis denied that any such offer was made, and if it had been it would have been in writing in case of illness or death.

There was much dirt thrown and plenty of sharp legal cut and thrust as you might expect when the cast included such names as Gilbert Beyfus, QC, the Grey Fox, for Lewis, and Gerald Gardiner, QC, later the Lord Chancellor, for Austin and his company. The case turned on who said what. Austin said at the meeting in 1956 Lewis told him that although Bolton West wanted him as their candidate, Morgan Phillips, then the secretary of the Labour party, and Lord Attlee, the former Prime Minister and leader of the party, would not have him at all. Lewis also talked of being big in business like Clore and Wolfson, the top names in finance at the time, and claimed that he ran the Coal Board and was responsible for the sacking of the chairman and the appointment of the man who replaced him.

Austin, who had gone round to ask Lewis to sponsor him to join the Royal Automobile Club in Piccadilly, said Lewis 'was full of his usual arrogance. He made some far-reaching claims about his association with the National Coal Board.' Austin said he had heard it all before and wanted to restore some sanity to the conversation. It was then that Lewis made the offer.

Lewis flatly denied it all. He said that Austin's statements were a malicious (a word that was always around when Lewis was in action) invention to harm his business and his relationship with the Coal Board and others.

At the end of four days of evidence the judge, Mr Justice Barry, went away to think about it and when he returned four days later to give his judgment he explained the delay. He said that he was not overwhelmingly impressed by the accounts of either Lewis or Austin so he had had to look elsewhere for the answer. In one respect this was unfortunate, because it raised an apparently irreconcilable conflict between the evidence of two businessmen who were for five years colleagues in the same party in the House of Commons, well acquainted but not on close or social terms. For this reason, the judge said, the case perhaps assumed an importance greater than the amount of money at stake would merit.

The judge said he had to look for corroboration. In Austin's case there was none, and his account was positively contradicted by every other witness called, either by him or by Lewis. For that reason, he found for Lewis, with costs, and rejected Austin's irrelevant account of Lewis making derogatory remarks about people alive or dead and connected with the Coal Board. He thought Austin possessed a somewhat lively imagination. But at the same time he did not necessarily accept every word of Lewis's evidence against Austin. He said that Lewis was rather impatient with views which did not accord with his own, and in particular he was apt to deny with very great emphasis the existence or possible existence of any facts which he himself did not clearly recall.

Lewis left the court well pleased with the result. He was not so pleased with the share price of his company. Shares had fallen from 22 shillings (now 110p) in 1957 to 7 shillings and 4 pence (37p) by the end of 1958, and he needed fresh capital injected into his ailing company.

On 23 December, 1958, the *Daily Mail* and the *Daily Telegraph* both ran short stories on their front pages which said almost the same, that officers of the City of London Fraud Squad were inquiring into the affairs of Rubber Improvement Ltd whose chairman was John Lewis, a former socialist MP. Lewis was not having that. He considered it was a serious libel and promptly sued. It was over two years before the case came to court.

However, in March 1959, Lewis was again in the High Court, suing over a racehorse called Hamama who had a heart attack in the 1956 2,000 Guineas. Lewis, who had paid £7,000 for the three-year-old less than a fortnight before, stopped the cheque and later ordered the horse to be destroyed, which caused a great deal of comment. Lewis had an answer for that.

It was a case that ran for days, attracting full houses with some turned away because it had all the ingredients for a smash hit: famous names, horse racing and drama. The expensive legal line-up included several up-and-coming barristers soon to be judges, such as Fred Lawton, Michael Eastham and Helenus Milmo and the Grey Fox too. Beyfus was appearing for the former owners of the horse: Prince Tousson, cousin of King Farouk of Egypt; the Prince's trainer and sometime business partner Jack Cunnington, one of the leading French trainers, who had run a stables at Chantilly since 1922, and his wife Marguerite, because in French law husband and wife shared everything.

The horse, Hamama, who had had some good races in France as a two-year-old in 1955, beating the 1956 Derby winner Lavadin in his last outing, had one problem, and that was in his breeding. It made no difference to the gambler, but for the breeder there was a definite blank in his pedigree. He was missing a maternal grandmother, because the dam had been foaled and bred in Germany during the Second World War. After the invasion of France valuable racehorses were stolen as well as art treasures.

Lewis bought the horse – after being assured that he was in

perfect condition – to be trained by Sir Gordon Richards, who had been champion jockey a record twenty-six times before retiring to train, for the 2,000 Guineas. Lewis promised £5,000 in addition to the selling price if the horse won.

But Hamama, ridden by Billy Rickaby, had a disastrous race. He was all right for three furlongs and then, to the astonishment of the jockey, trainer and Lewis, began to sway around as if drunk and finished a disappointing and bad last.

Subsequent examination showed that the horse had a heart defect and after some time at the Equine Research Station at Newmarket, Lewis ordered it to be destroyed in October 1956. He said in evidence that he did this after he had ordered that the horse be given graduated exercise for six months. After that he was told that the horse would not fetch much as a four-year-old with a suspicious heart and for humanitarian reasons Lewis ordered him to be put down. He said the experts always wanted a horse to live, but they did not have to pay the bills. Many of the vets, who followed trainers, jockeys and other experts through the witness box, disagreed and said the horse should have been given a longer chance. The only vet who thought Lewis had acted correctly was Sir Winston Churchill's manager.

After all the evidence the judge, Mr Justice Paull, went away for nine days to think about it, because he admitted the case was giving him a good deal of trouble. When he returned to give his ninety-minute judgment he started by saying that a horse was sound in law if it was fit to do the job intended, and in this case that meant racing. You did not warrant that the horse had a heart which would remain sound during racing or that the horse was so strongly built that it was unlikely to break down at a future date. The warranty, he ruled, was that at the moment of sale the horse's heart was not diseased and the horse was fit for the kind of work the person who bought it intended. The real difficulty was to define exactly what was meant by those words in the case of a racehorse, because it was only comparatively recently that it had been recognized that a horse which from its appearance and performance was apparently sound in heart might in fact have a diseased one. The judge said that he had had a look at the reference book, *Oliphant on Horses*, and although 105 diseases were mentioned, the heart was not referred to at all.

Until recently, tests on horses' hearts had been limited to

checking the condition before and after exercise with a stetho-scope, but now there was the Equine Research Station where horses could be kept under observation for many days with constant examination by electrocardiographs. It had been dis-covered that a heart could be dilated by a hard race, but the next day would return to normal.

He said that Lewis's case was that the horse strained his heart in the three races before the sale. The Prince and the Cunningtons said there were several possible explanations for the breakdown in the race. The judge's view was that Hamama's heart strain existed before the date of sale and that it was not sound in the sense that it could not reasonably be expected to undergo the strain of racing in the Guineas without breaking down.

When a leading French vet examined the horse before the sale, he did not discover the defect – and this was no criticism of any of the vets who gave evidence – because modern science had shown that it was not enough to listen to the heart with a stethoscope. He gave judgment for Lewis, stressing that there was no question of bad faith on anyone's part, even though he had to find a breach of warranty.

The judge's decision meant that Lewis had to pay the true value of Hamama on the day of sale which – and it was pure speculation – was 500 guineas. Lewis was entitled to his counter claim of £750 for such matters as the cost of the horse for twelve weeks and his commission to the agency through whom he bought the horse. Lewis in turn had to pay the agency their commission of £420. The case cost around £15,000 in legal fees, double the price Lewis paid for the horse. The judge made an order that Lewis should recover much of his.

Lewis said afterwards that although he was delighted he was more pleased that the horse's heart trouble had led to the discovery of other similar cases. Before Hamama was put down the Equine Research Staion had had only one case in ten years.

Lewis carried on racing and socializing. His business troubles were becoming worse which worried him a great deal. He was making no progress in his bid to get back into the mainstream of politics. He was still complaining about Ward to those who would listen, saying what he would like to do to him, how he would get him one day. He had been saying it throughout the fifties and he was saying it as the new decade, which was to revolutionize outlooks on sex and morals, began.

8

PROFUMO AND KEELER

In 1961 certain events occurred which on their own were interesting, but when put in the context of what happened later, were vitally important. At the time they either made great headlines or occurred in private and were known only to a select few.

At the beginning of the year Ward had another exhibition at a gallery in St James showing his chalk studies of royalty, politicians such as Macmillan, Home Secretary Rab Butler, Foreign Secretary Selwyn Lloyd and Labour leader Hugh Gaitskell, and such notables as Paul Getty and Nubar Gulbenkian. The exhibition was a great success.

On 7 January the Portland spy ring was broken. This was a successful, Russian-organized operation in which secrets from the submarine base at Portland in Dorset were sold by an embittered petty officer who used his girl-friend to help deliver them to their contact man, Gordon Lonsdale. He was a very smooth spy who in turn took the minute pictures to a house in Ruislip where they were transmitted to Moscow by a very ordinary couple called Kroger who had done vital work in getting their masters atomic secrets, under the cover of an antique book business. MI5, with the aid of Special Branch, mounted a watching operation once they got on to Lonsdale, who was a colonel in the KGB. They used the house opposite the Krogers' in a normal suburban street. Apart from the value of the counter-espionage operation, there was considerable drama in the human side of the story, involving the use of the house of decent, normal people, who regarded the Krogers as their best friends. The dilemma and the effect on the couple is brilliantly told in Hugh Whitemore's play *A Pack of Lies*, which faithfully records what happened.

The British couple, Houghton and Gee, were gaoled for fifteen years and on release married and lived on the south coast.

The Krogers got twenty years each and Lonsdale twenty-five. The Russians did not have to complete their sentences. They were exchanged for British agents who had been captured in Russia and held for such a purpose. The Portland case ended on 22 March, and less than two months later a bigger spy was gaoled at the Old Bailey for forty-two years, which is still a British record. George Blake was a double-double agent and he was not exchanged. He was helped to escape and he made it back to Russia where he is still living (1992).

Neither of these cases were good news for the government and a special committee was set up under Lord Radcliffe to look at spying, and another to enquire into prison security. While all this was going on another British spy was working away for the Russians, a naval clerk called William Vassall. His activities, which were to lead him to prison in 1962, the effect of the Radcliffe report and the inquiry following the Vassall affair all led to considerable government annoyance at the press and the criticism it voiced over the regular discovery of spies. All this blew into a terrible, unforgiving battle when the Profumo Affair broke open.

On 20 January Ward was introduced to Captain Eugene Ivanov, the Russian naval attaché, who had been in London since 27 March 1960. It was the start of a good relationship and friendship because the two men liked each other and spent a lot of time in each other's company. Ward taught Ivanov to play bridge and introduced him to Spring Cottage, which Lord 'Bill' Astor had lent him for a peppercorn rent in the grounds of his home at Cliveden on the Thames since 1956. It was a good arrangement. Cliveden, once the meeting place for the anti-war faction before the Second World War, was the Astor family home and a great gathering place for house parties every weekend in the fifties and early sixties. The cottage in the grounds which Ward had converted was a fun place and everyone wanted to go there. 'It was a funday Sunday there when London was boring. Stephen always had such a good crowd there, including pretty girls,' one visitor recalls. The pretty girls were one of the attractions for Bill Astor, who was a good friend and patient of Ward. He also liked sex and Ward not only massaged away his ills, but provided the means of easing other instincts.

When Ward and Ivanov met in January it was another thread towards the climax. The two were introduced by the then editor of the *Daily Telegraph* Sir Colin Coote, who was a patient of Ward and knew of his left-wing leanings and his wish to meet Russians in order to draw them. Coote had met Ivanov at a party and introduced him to several people.

What neither the host nor Ward knew then was that Ivanov was much more than an ordinary naval attaché. He was working for the KGB, and there are many now who think that his real role was to infiltrate British society, which he did very well, and to use this entrée to hit the British government in every possible way.

His warm personality and love of fun and parties – he was host of his own parties with his wife Maya and a good guest at other parties on his own – went down well with the Ward set. Ward particularly appreciated having him around. It was to be his way into the Russian world in London and then in Moscow where he planned to take his British portfolio to Khrushchev, the Russian leader, and ask if he could draw him. But what was to have been just a contact friendship became a genuine one and for a while the two men were inseparable, arguing politics, Ivanov taking Ward to the Russian Embassy parties, Ward taking Ivanov to his and introducing him to his girls.

In June the government became worried about the sabre-rattling by the then leader of Iraq, General Kassem, against the tiny shiekdom of Kuwait. It was a similar act by Saddam Hussein in 1991 that led to the rest of the world taking up arms against him because he actually carried out his threat and invaded Kuwait, so oil rich and so vital to our interests. Kassem in 1961 did not actually invade Kuwait but it was such a strong threat that on 30 June the top secret order was given that 6,000 British troops should go to Kuwait and be ready for action.

It was the first test of the new type of answer to an emergency, a fighting force that could go quickly to deal with a limited brush-fire war. It was an antidote to the fiasco of the Suez operation in 1956 which brought humiliation for Britain and brought about the end of Sir Anthony Eden's short premiership.

The Kuwait operation seemed to be a success. Kassem backed off and the troops prepared to come home. The Minister of Defence, Harold Watkinson, said in a speech on 8 July that it was a model of what British forces were doing in the modern world to fulfil their obligations to keep the peace.

However, it was not quite what it appeared, and soon there were to be complaints to the man who kept an eagle eye on military matters for the Labour party, Colonel George Wigg, a professional soldier for many years. He was to get letters about the lack of drinking water, poor food and wrong medical advice. It was not for another year that he could be sure, because the government report on the medical aspects of the operation was not published until then.

So, already, there were three stories coming in like spokes to a hub: there was the growing hatred between government and press over spying, there was the friendship between Ivanov and Ward and their link with Cliveden, and there was the potential clash between Colonel Wigg and the Secretary of State, John Profumo, known to many as Jack.

The next stop, the vital event which was to help Lewis in his attempt to pay Ward back (although he knew nothing of it for over a year), happened in the grounds of Cliveden over the weekend of 8/9 July 1961.

There was a house party at the big house and among the thirty guests were the President of Pakistan and the Profumos: John, the Secretary of State, relaxing from the worries of the Kuwait crisis which was to end later when Kassem gave way and the troops came home, and his lovely wife, Valerie Hobson, former film star. She had been starring in *The King and I* when they were married in January 1954. She had the classic cool beauty of the English aristocrat, and looked every inch one. She gave up acting when she married. She has been a wonderful wife, sticking loyally to her husband ever since, despite all the disgrace and misery he brought upon himself and her.

But on that weekend at Cliveden, when the weather was as perfect as it can ever be in Britain, the glittering prizes were beckoning John Dennis Profumo. He came from a Sardinian family who had emigrated to Britain in 1885, built their fortunes on insurance and had fitted into society with wealth and charm. His father was a baron and a King's Counsel and the family home was a mansion just outside Stratford-upon-Avon in Warwickshire. Young John went to Harrow and to Brasenose College, Oxford (and one of the reasons why top Tories believed his lies later was that the Attorney-General Sir John Hobson (who was to die from a brain tumour), was at Harrow, and Brasenose, Oxford and in the same regiment with him), before working very actively in politics. He was chairman of the Tory association in East Fulham at the age of twenty-two, where the then MP (another coincidence) was Bill Astor.

Profumo's reward was to be selected as candidate for Kettering and he became the youngest MP in the House of Commons when he · was elected in 1940. His friends and admirers predicted that one day he would become Prime Minister and it was a possibility. He had been a serving officer in the Army for six months when he was elected, choosing the Army rather than the Royal Air Force to the surprise of his friends, because he was an accomplished flyer. He showed political courage almost immediately by becoming one of the thirty Tory MPs (who included Macmillan, Bob Boothby and Quintin Hogg, later Lord Hailsham and Lord Chancellor) who voted against Chamberlain, thus making way for Churchill to take over as Prime Minister and war leader.

Profumo had a good war. He was a brilliant organizer, charming, hard working, rather a ladies' man, and a good MP; he made a memorable speech in 1944, flying back from Italy where he was on Field Marshal Alexander's staff, to call for leave for men serving in the Far East and the Mediterranean and for an increase in the clothing allowance for serving women. He was handsome, he was lithe, smooth, slightly balding and highly attractive to women.

After the war he lost his seat, like many Tories. He stayed on as Chief of Staff of the British liaison team in Japan, working with General Douglas MacArthur and reaching the rank of brigadier before coming out of the Army and becoming one of Rab Butler's backroom boys in Tory Central Office. He got back into Parliament in 1950 as MP for Stratford-upon-Avon, literally his old hunting ground (a sport he had given up by then). He had his first government job in 1952, working his way ever upwards until Macmillan made him Secretary of State for War in July 1960, with a brief to get 165,000 men for the Army by 1963 following the end of conscription. It was a job that suited this coming man with a flair for PR and headline catching speeches, and the necessary skill in advertising to make the Army sound an exciting life, a cut above the kind of job a young man would find in civvy street. He made a success of it.

So all was well, apart from the slight cloud over Kuwait, and the future exciting and promising as Profumo, his wife, Bill Astor and all his guests wandered down to the swimming pool in evening dress after dinner on a balmy, still night.

The sight that met Profumo's eyes would warm the heart and other parts of any warm-blooded man. In the water and just coming out was a superb girl, long-legged, doe-eyed, with flowing chestnut hair; but much, much better than that: she was nude and showing off her magnificent body. The girl was moulded in the image that Dr Ward liked to build for his girls, who were mostly straight from the provinces and looking for their fame and fortune in London. She had exciting breasts and a figure that made some catch their breath with delight.

She was Christine Keeler, aged nineteen and she was down for the day. A friend had given her a lift in his car for the thirty-mile journey from London. She was one of Ward's house guests, even though she was living with him in a brother-sister relationship, sleeping together but never having sex. The rest of Ward's guests were at the pool too, because Bill Astor was quite happy for him and his friends to use it. It was part of the strange relationship that Astor and Ward had.

Before the party from the big house arrived, there had been some horseplay and Ward had grabbed Christine's costume and thrown it into the bushes. Before she could get out and retrieve it, Astor's group had sauntered down with cigars and brandy balloons to see what all the fun was about. There was much splashing and shouting and giggling as Christine came out of the water naked like a nymh and tried to grab a soaking towel, which was replaced later by the thoughtful Mrs Profumo. She, like the other ladies, was in an exquisite long gown. Christine then went to get her costume, but Profumo and Astor tried to stop her and for a couple of minutes or so they played a game of chase with the naked girl before allowing her to get her costume back and put it on. The two panting middle-aged men watched with lust. It was difficult for Christine to dress. The towel was too small and she had to wriggle and struggle and in the light of the moon Profumo watched her. Then Ward turned on the floodlights and everything reverted to normal. Astor, the perfect host, introduced Ward who already knew Profumo, and the others and then invited the Ward party up to the house for drinks. They went and it was Profumo who showed Keeler around the house, laughing and chatting her up. He even made a grab for her in fun and helped dress her in a suit of armour; he laughed with the others as she clanked around the hall.

The tour ended with Christine saying that she had to get back to London so that she could show some other friends the way down in the morning. Bill Astor asked the Ward crowd to come and have a lunchtime, poolside picnic. Profumo was pleased. He was much taken with this little darling who, despite the occasion and the importance of Astor's guests, did not lose the charm and poise that Ward had taught her.

The guest for whom Christine returned to London introduced the next chapter in the story that was to end in disaster. He was the jovial Russian spy, Eugene Ivanov, and they arrived when the pool party was in full flow, with nearly everyone in swimsuits with a glass in hand. Ward introduced the Russian, who was persuaded to take part in the swimming races Bill Astor was arranging. It was a curious situation because Astor must have known that Penkovsky, a former Soviet military intelligence colonel who had defected earlier in the year and spilled big cans of secrets to his new masters, had told MI5 that Ivanov was not just a naval attaché but a spy. MI5 had been to see Ward and told him they knew of his association with Ivanov; they did not mind, but if anything happened that might interest them would he get in touch? Some accounts suggest that it was Ward who made the offer, but whoever it was, Ward agreed to the plan. It is almost certain that Bill Astor, a wartime naval intelligence officer, would have been given the nod about what was going on by his friends in the security services.

So there they were lining up for the race of the afternoon: the Secretary of State for War and the Russian spy, who had already been asking Ward about the timing of the delivery of nuclear warheads to West Germany, and was considered by MI5 as a possible candidate for turning to the British side. There were others in the race, including the President of Pakistan, and there was only one rule: they could use any arm stroke they liked but their feet were not to touch the ground. The Russian and the Pakistani were in the lead in the one-length race until the closing stages at the shallow end, when Profumo put his feet on the ground and got home by a touch. There were protests that he should be disqualified, but he said with a grin: 'That'll teach you to trust a Minister of the Crown.' It was a jest, but nearly two years later the truth behind the warning became clear.

The swimming race was followed by mock jousting and each man had a girl on his shoulder. The girl on Profumo's shoulders was Christine, simmering and fabulously sexual in her one-piece black swimsuit. Photographs were taken, of the minister and the girl, groups with Ward and his girls, Profumo, Ivanov and Astor and the girls. The permutations were many as the guests at the party took it in turns to snap away in the sunshine amidst the poolside picnic and drinks.

Late in the afternoon Ward asked Ivanov to drive Christine back to London because he had to give Bill Astor a massage. Ward said he would join him later and go to the club they used in Edgware Road in west London. It was one of Ward's regular haunts where he played bridge, had a drink and a meal and cashed cheques.

Ivanov agreed. He and Christine went back in the late afternoon light traffic. The flat was empty on their return because by now Ward's other current girl from the provinces, Mandy Rice-Davies, had gone. She had come to London at the age of fifteen to be a model at the motor show at Earls Court. Later she worked at the respectable Murray's Club in the West End, where she met Christine Keeler. For a while they had a great time, living for a while at Ward's flat in Bryanton Mews, (the one in which Hamilton and Rachman had romped the days and nights away) sleeping around, and then falling under Rachman's spell. Keeler had lived with him for a few months at the end of 1959 and early in 1960 but Rachman, who was generous but extremely jealous, found out that she was seeing a boyhood sweetheart and dumped her. It was typical of him that he should allow her to keep the clothes and gifts he had given her. On the afternoon of the 9 July when Ivanov, whom Keeler later described as a 'wonderful huggy bear of a man', drove her back to London, Mandy was living with Rachman.

Mandy was different from Keeler. Originally from Birmingham, she had buttermilk skin and dairy curls, a pert nose and a cheeky face, and she frankly did not give a damn, not even for red-robed judges and stern magistrates, as she was later to show.

So the Ward flat was empty when the Russian bear and the showgirl pulled up outside and Ivanov took a bottle of vodka from the boot of his Zis Soviet car, they went inside and Keeler put the kettle on. They drank tea mixed with vodka and then just vodka.

Keeler was already a happy girl. Shortly before they had left Cliveden, Profumo had asked her for her phone number. She did not give it to him directly even though she was thrilled at the idea of having an affair with a minister of the Crown, husband of a beautiful former film star. Profumo had already made a pass at her, and the idea of going further excited her. She was under no illusions that theirs would be a platonic friendship, and knowing that his interest lay entirely between the sheets aroused her. Nevertheless she did not tell him her number. She told him to ask Ward, for she knew that Ward would give it to him. In any case, it was the number they shared at Ward's flat.

She did not tell the Russian this as they drank and talked and then, as such matters normally proceed, they started cuddling and kissing. As they drank more vodka the reluctant Russian's inhibitions began to disappear, although he was really a moral man who was not normally unfaithful to his wife. They went to bed. If Ward had returned, things might have been different. He did not. He stayed at the party and had given Profumo the girl's phone number. The news quickly got around their circle, but there was very little reaction, because girls and men got together like that all the time and everyone knew about Bill Astor and his friends.

Ivanov was sad when their love-making was over. He drank more vodka in his misery that he had betrayed his wife and his country, and although Keeler did all she could to make him feel better he left in a drunken, morose state.

Much happened in the next two weeks. On the Tuesday after the Cliveden weekend Profumo rang Keeler and asked her to meet him. Their affair was short and very sweet; they slept together a few times, once in the Profumo matrimonial bed. He took her around, usually in his little red Mini but once in a borrowed official car, not telling the fellow minister from whom he had borrowed it what he was up to. It was for lust, and Profumo satisfied it with a willing partner. The fact that the affair lasted for so short a time shows that Profumo was a careful man. He tried to make sure, for instance, that Ward did not know what was going on, although of course Ward did. As they snuggled up at night Ward and Keeler told each other their secrets and neither was discreet. They always talked about what was going on, and with Ward's hobby and habit of dropping names, the more famous the better, everything was known.

Four days after the Cliveden weekend, Ward had another visit from his personal watchdog from MI5. It showed that they were worried that Ivanov was mixing in society so easily and so quickly. They knew that the Secretary of State had met Ivanov at an embassy function for spaceman Yuri Gagarin on the Tuesday, but they did not know that he knew him socially as well. The second visit was to find out what Ivanov was talking about, whom he was meeting, where he was going, what his views were. They knew he had been around and about with Ward and were happy for this to be encouraged, but were troubled by the wider circle of acquaintances to whom Ward was introducing him.

The visit produced a piece of information that was not expected. Ward just could not help himself (he had a childish, naughty-boy trick of making the most indiscreet remarks, spilling nasty gossip in front of the victim, and then giggling; a form of cover like master spy Kim Philby's stammer), and he had to tell that he knew the Secretary of State Jack Profumo. For once he kept his mouth shut about the fact that Profumo was having sex with Keeler.

Profumo, dealing with the planned withdrawal of the troops from Kuwait once Kassem had backed off, did not know of this for a while. He was enjoying himself with the girl, having her whenever he could but not knowing that she was the confidante of Ward. Ward thought he had been recruited by MI5, a belief he held to the end. It was a reasonable assumption because that is what MI5 wanted him to believe, and he was certainly no traitor. He did what he could to provide information on what Ivanov was after, particularly when it came to nuclear warheads.

What he did not know for sure and nor did anyone else until 1992, was that Ivanov was working for GRU, the main intelligence directorate of the Soviet Army, linked in the network under the KGB. He claims that it was Sir Colin Coote who provided him with an entry into the social circles in which the elite mixed, without which he could not have succeeded as a spy. In his autobiography he makes other claims about his espionage activities like photographing 'secret papers' on Bill Astor's desk at Cliveden, looking through Sir Winston Churchill's private papers while visiting his home when Ward was treating him, acquaintanceship with some of the royal family, possession of unspecified secret information about them which is lodged in the archives of the GRU for future use and providing the Motherland with insider information from a social contact that the exchange rate was to be reviewed, netting millions of roubles for the Russian exchequer. None of this was known or suspected at the time and is new, untested but fascinating information.

9

THE LEWIS LIBEL CASE

Just eleven days after Profumo met Keeler and started his affair, Lewis, knowing absolutely nothing about it, went to the High Court to sue the *Daily Telegraph* and the *Daily Mail* for the libel which he claimed they committed on 23 December 1958, on the front page of their papers.

His company was in trouble at the time. On 19 July 1961, it needed an urgent injection of capital for which he had searched high and low without success. Friends and contacts came up with ideas, but no cash. The two small stories that Lewis claimed meant he was guilty of fraud were almost the same. In the *Daily Telegraph*, which was sued first in front of the usual extremely expensive legal gentlemen and, for once, a jury, the story said:

> *Inquiry on Firm by City Police*
> Officers of the City of London Fraud Squad are inquiring into the affairs of Rubber Improvement Ltd and its subsidiary companies. The investigation was requested after criticism of the chairman's statement and the accounts by a shareholder at the recent Company meeting.
>
> The Chairman of the Company, which has an authorized capital of £1 mil., is Mr John Lewis, former Socialist MP for Bolton.

The *Daily Mail* story said:

> *Fraud Squad Probes Firm*
> The City Fraud Squad under Superintendent Francis Lea is inquiring into the affairs of Rubber Improvement Ltd. Chairman

of the company whose shares have dropped from 22/- last year to 7/4d yesterday, is Mr John Lewis, former Socialist MP.

The company specializes in flexible rubber conveyor belting designed for the National Coal Board.

It had taken thirty months for the case to come to the High Court. The *Telegraph* case lasted two days and it revolved around what the ordinary man, on reading the article, thought it meant. Lewis claimed that by innuendo the article meant that the company's affairs and those of its subsidiaries were conducted fraudulently or dishonestly, because it was generally known that the City Fraud Squad investigate serious cases of company fraud. And, Lewis claimed, it also implied that he had been guilty or was suspected of fraud or dishonesty and had let his company affairs be conducted fraudulently or dishonestly. He told the jury: 'Millions of people would immediately think that there is no smoke without fire. At no time was there an investigation into the company's affairs.'

There was a letter from the Commissioner of Police in August 1960 which referred to an investigation carried out by the fraud department, but stating it was not proposed to start any criminal proceedings as a result of them.

Lewis, a smartly dressed and excellently articulate witness, said that a report containing words like 'fraud' and the name of the chairman was sufficient to put in anyone's mind that something was rotten in the 'state of Denmark'. When a story like that appeared in a newspaper, in ninety-nine cases out of a hundred there was subsequently a prosecution.

The *Daily Telegraph*'s defence was that in its ordinary meaning the article was true, and they denied the innuendoes. They also said in mitigation of damages, without denying that they had been defamatory, that they had printed the next day Lewis's view of the facts and that he was also suing the *Daily Mail*.

Neville Faulks, QC, later a judge, told the jury that the paper's view was that the report meant that the police were merely doing their job and did not suspect anyone. The paper had done only a piece of accurate reporting, as it was entitled to.

The judge, Mr Justice Salmon, said the case largely depended on what the words meant to the ordinary man. There were two views: the *Telegraph*'s counsel said that the ordinary man was not unduly suspicious, but the counsel for Lewis said that the ordinary man, seeing the article, would immediately say that there is either fraud here or at least enough for the police to suspect fraud. If, the judge went on, the words meant what Lewis said they did, it was difficult to think of anything that would do the company more harm to them in business. The judge left it to the jury to decide what this 'ordinary man' would make of it all, and to use their commonsense when assessing any damages.

The jury came back after almost two hours to ask about the movement of Rubber Improvement's shares in the ten days after the publication of the *Telegraph* report, but were told that neither side had called evidence on that point, a lapse which was to be rectified in the *Mail* trial.

Twenty minutes later they were back, and five minutes later Lewis could have been forgiven for having another heart attack. They awarded Lewis £25,000 damages, an exceptionally large sum for those days. Then they announced the damages for his company, an astonishing, outstanding, record-breaking £75,000. It was a lifeline, a tax-free bonanza which was totally unexpected. Lewis went out to celebrate, knowing that the next day he was in line for a Monte Carlo jackpot.

The same legal cast lined up for the *Mail* case and the story was similar, with one major exception: Associated Newspapers, who owned both the *Daily Mail* and the now defunct *Evening News*, had already paid 500 guineas' damages to Lewis (who donated it to the Cancer Research Fund) for the same libel in the *Evening News* on 23 December 1958. There was also another point. When the *Daily Mail* reporter rang Lewis he at first thought it was a practical joke; when he discovered it was not, he warned the reporter that if any report appeared linking him or his company with the Fraud Squad, writs would be issued immediately.

Lewis told the jury: 'I made it clear that it was quite untrue and that at no time had anyone approached us with regard to any such matter. I used different, rather strong language. I regret that I said "I will drag you on your belly before one of Her Majesty's judges if you print any of this nonsense".'

The *Mail*'s defence was that of the *Telegraph*, that in its ordinary meaning the story was true and they denied any innuendoes. They also made the point that the share price had gone up after the story was printed, and that Lewis had never mentioned the alleged libel at his annual shareholders' meetings since publication.

Lewis said that within two years of the report the company, which had been making a profit, had a loss of £430,000. It was not all due to the libel but a very substantial amount was.

The judge started his summing up by telling the jury that they were not to be influenced by the damages awarded in the *Telegraph* case and should approach the case with entirely fresh minds. Making the same points as on the day before, he said that if the report carried the meaning Lewis said it did, it constituted a very serious libel. He spoke of the serious fall-off in business in Rubber Improvement in the year before the report appeared, the shares dropping from 21 shillings (105p) to about 7 shillings (35p), how they had dropped another shilling (5p) after the libel but a few days later had gained a shilling or so. The shares at the time of the trial were worth 3 shillings and 6 pence (17½p).

The jury were out for only about an hour this time. They topped the *Telegraph* award comfortably, setting a new record for damages which has only become commonplace in the late eighties and early nineties. For Lewis, who had said during the course of the trial that he personally wanted only an apology, there was £17,000. For his company there was £100,000, a truly enormous and amazing sum. It meant he had been awarded a total of £217,000, an injection of tax-free capital which could be the company's salvation. He sat there, his face wreathed in smiles, a very happy and contented man.

It was, of course, too good to be completely true. Both papers promptly appealed. As Lewis waited the long months before the appeal was heard, the Profumo Affair was in full heat. Once MI5 knew that the minister was mixing in the same circles as a suspected Russian spy (but not knowing that both men were sharing the favours of the same girl), an urgent meeting was held. The Director-General Sir Roger Hollis, himself later to be falsely accused of being a Russian spy, went to see the Cabinet Secretary, Sir (later Lord) Norman Brook, told him what they knew, and asked him to have a quiet word with Profumo. There was nothing against him, but they thought he should know about Ivanov and the link between the two of them and Ward.

It was only thirty-two days after he had met Keeler that Profumo saw the Cabinet Secretary. The interview was man to

man, a friendly warning but with a sting in the tail. The Cabinet
Secretary told the Secretary of State that MI5 was watching
Ivanov and had noticed that Profumo was an acquaintance of
both the Russian and Ward. Would he (Profumo) be prepared
to act for MI5, perhaps have a word with Ivanov, see if he was a
chap for turning? Profumo did not hesitate. He said no, he
wanted no part of anything like that. Brook understood at once.
He let that line drop immediately and instead suggested to
Profumo that it might be a good idea if he stayed away from the
Ward group because the surveillance and the operation to turn
the Russian would continue. MI5 thought this was a possibility,
although there were others in MI6 who thought than Ivanov had
been planted to get into society and to mix with politicians and
top people in the hope of causing embarrassment and trouble. If
that was the aim he had some success, not so much because he
engineered it, but because Lewis prodded and poked and lit the
fuse.

Profumo suggested that all Cabinet members who knew Ward
and his crowd should also be warned about the operation to turn
Ivanov, so that they could keep well away. Profumo must have
been a very relieved man when he left the Secretary's office,
because there had been no mention of his affair with Keeler. It
was clear that MI5 did not know, had not even noticed, because
they were watching the Russian, not the politician. Keeler was
just a girl who was around Ward's flat; she had been seen when
Ward's case officer called, but she had not been introduced.
MI5 knew a great deal about Ward, his leftish sympathies, his
way of life, but not his sex life in detail. That did not interest
them.

So Profumo was free to carry on his relationship with Keeler.
But he was a clever man. He had been given a clear warning that
there would be problems if he went on mixing in the Ward
group. He had already asked Keeler to move out and planned to
set her up in a flat, but she did not want to do that. Profumo,
who had already been uneasy about the Ward set-up, now did
his best to avoid him. Ward had been at the Russian embassy
party for Gagarin with Ivanov and he was always about when
Profumo picked up Keeler from the flat. Ivanov was also about,
although they did not meet and by that time (although Profumo
did not know it) they were not sharing the same woman. Once
was enough for the guilt-ridden, highly moral Russian who was

concerned about such matters when it came to his personal life but for whom espionage activities were perfectly acceptable.

These were some of the disadvantages for Profumo of carrying on with the girl who so fascinated him. There was another, but he was not to know that for nearly two years. Ward, in his friendly Russian hat, no doubt prompted by his friend, had asked Keeler to question Jack as they lay in bed about when Germany was going to get the nuclear warheads. Ward, who had already joked that Keeler would be ruling the world next, as she was sleeping with two such important people, may have been joking, or he may not have been; but Keeler never asked the question. Perhaps if she had done so it might have given all the fuss later some credence.

The advantage of carrying on with the nymphet who was so good in bed was just that; she was a wonderful lay and nothing else. Profumo weighed up the situation and decided that it was time to pull out. He knew there were photographs but they included many people so there was nothing compromising there. Then he did a very foolish thing. He wrote a note on War Office paper.

It said:

Darling – in great haste because I can get no reply from your phone – Alas something's blown up tomorrow night and I can't therefore make it. I'm terribly sorry especially as I have to leave the next day for various trips and then a holiday so won't be able to see you again until some time in September. Blast it. Please take great care of yourself and don't run away.
   Love J.
P.S. I'm writing this cos I know you're off for the day tomorrow and I want you to know before you go if I still can't reach you by phone.

And that was it. He did not see her again and as far as he was concerned that was the end. She regarded it as the end too, and probably thought very little about it. There were other men to meet and it was the eve of the move towards a new world, suggested and organized by Ward.

Lewis and Wigg, who still had not come into the action, because there was none, were busy men. Lewis was socializing, racing, hating, trying to save his business and find favour again, (with no luck) with the Labour party. Colonel Wigg, long-time ordinary soldier before being commissioned in the war, a very good Labour MP for Dudley and a man not to be crossed, was learning that all had not gone as the War Office claimed during the Kuwait operation. It was over by mid-summer and the soldiers were home, but there were disturbing stories of dehydration; it was also rumoured that many men were not fit to fight because no-one had bothered to prepare them. Wigg set to work to find out those who were responsible.

Strangely, he shared with Ward a history of beatings at school which were to influence his thinking in adult life. Wigg had won a scholarship to a Hampshire grammar school and no boy ever went to school more willingly. He came from a poor family with a strong background history but at what he was to call a 'twentieth century version of Charles Dickens' Dotheboys Hall' he found a snobbish heavy-drinking clergyman who sneered at scholarship boys and caned them mercilessly. He never forgot the pain and humiliation the headmaster inflicted on him, an eager pupil who had the misfortune to come from the wrong side of the track.

Wigg was a fine man but he never forgot a slight.

10

TIME LAG

Before the affair blew open there was a silence and a terribly long wait. There was a long wait because nothing significant had happened and no action need ever have been taken. There had been a quick affair between a politician and a girl, and there had been an even quicker affair between the girl and a Russian who was certainly a spy. MI5 were watching the spy whom they strongly suspected of being in Britain to stir up trouble; they were right about that, but were hardly likely to mention it to anyone. The evidence of the entire affair is that they kept silent as much as they possibly could and would never have said anything if they had not been forced by the circumstances, which were brought about by Lewis. After all, that was the whole point of the existence of MI5, to keep things quiet for the good of the State.

In August 1961, soon after Profumo slept with Keeler for the last time, the East Germans sealed the border with the west in Berlin and a few days later began building the Berlin Wall. It was the start of a period of Cold War activity that reached the very brink of nuclear war in October 1962. If the Cuban missile threat had been taken one step too far by either John Kennedy, who had become the youngest president of the United States in January 1961, or by Khruschev the aggressive Russian leader, it would have meant devastation, death, and a nuclear winter from which the world might never have recovered. Already 1961 had seen the Bay of Pigs invasion of Cuba which nearly overthrew Castro and created international tension of a kind not known since Hitler. Kennedy, who stood no nonsense from anyone and was extremely popular, held his ground.

For Lewis business went on with a great worry hanging over it. Both the *Daily Telegraph* and the *Daily Mail* asked for a stay of

79

execution while they considered whether to appeal. There was never any doubt. By the standards of those days (and these days) the awards by the jury were out of all proportion to what the papers had printed. As we know, the money would have been life blood for Lewis. The stay of execution was a terrible blow, but financially Lewis was all right. His gambling and astute investment saw to that. Yet it was a crushing kick to his vanity.

While all this was going on Ward was active sexually and also politically. In September, a month after Profumo had finished with Keeler whom Ward called 'little wicked baby' and who was still living with him, Ward got his old friend Bill Astor to write to the Foreign Office. The relationship between Ward and Astor was strong. The physiotherapist had been treating Astor as a patient since 1950, and had been his tenant since the day he spotted the cottage at Cliveden while on a trip on the Thames with his host. Astor had helped Ward financially to set up business with a loan which was repaid.

Astor most certainly did not share Ward's political views, his increasingly pro-Russian and Communist sympathies. But he was prepared to write the letter, in which he said that he had a friend called Stephen Ward who had become a friend of Ivanov and suggested that if the Foreign Office ever wanted to make sure that the Russian Embassy at any particular moment was correctly informed of western intentions, Ward was their man. He could pass on the information himself or arrange for the Russian Naval attaché to meet anyone. The letter was sent on 2 September and the Foreign Office acted quickly. On 18 September, just sixteen days later, a senior official interviewed Ward who gave a long account of his political views and his friendship with Ivanov, explaining how he wanted to use that friendship in a way which would be helpful to the Foreign Office. They said quite firmly that they did not want to use his services and probably thought that was the end of the matter. They did not know Ward, who thought he was already working for MI5.

He contacted one of his patients, Sir Godfrey Nicholson, a loyal Tory MP who had been so pleased with his treatment that he had recommended Ward to others. Ward decided that Sir Godfrey would be his best way into the Foreign Office. He told him that he wanted to get information for Ivanov about the British intentions of disarmament and Berlin as a means of promoting friendly relations between the two countries. Sir Godfrey went to see the Foreign Secretary who warned him that he should not meet Ivanov but Sir Godfrey told Lord Home (who two years later was to succeed Macmillan as Tory party leader and Prime Minister) that as an MP he must be free to talk to him. He wrote three letters to the Russian, long and detailed, all of which he cleared with the Foreign Office before sending them, via Ward, to Ivanov at the embassy. The two did not meet. It is ironical that the letters were delivered by Keeler, taken there by an unknowing friend in his car.

Still that was not enough for Ward. He went on and on at Sir Godfrey until he fixed a meeting with Sir Harold Caccia, the Permanent Under-Secretary of State at the Foreign Office. On 5 April 1962 they met for lunch. Ward offered to put Sir Harold directly in touch with Ivanov, but Sir Harold declined. The Foreign Office, oblivious of the MI5 game to try to turn Ivanov, and the even more sinister scam being operated by MI6 who were watching every move that Ivanov and Ward made, had their own strong reservations about Ward. He was not, after all, one of them.

Two more things happened before 1961 was out. The first involved Ward's descent to hell. He was still as interested as ever in the goings-on, normal and preferably perverted, of the fast set in which he lived and moved, but his taste buds were getting jaded. He needed something new to excite his palate. In the autumn he went down market, to the cafes and clubs of Notting Hill and Paddington, excited by the thought of coloured girls and drugs, the new swinging scene to be into – hash, marijuana and hemp. He would take Keeler down at night to watch the black prostitutes plying their trade. Secondly, from watching, Ward moved into visiting, so that one night Ward, Keeler and an artist friend went to a cafe in Notting Hill, where the riots had taken place a few years earlier, to try to buy some drugs. Ward sent Keeler to buy some and she came back successful, having also met a man who said he could supply a 'sister' for Ward to sleep with. Ward was delighted, but he would not have been if he had known what he had started. Another man they met in the cafe was Aloysius 'Lucky' Gordon, who was then thirty, having come from the West Indies thirteen years before. Ward, who did not want to lose any contact with his new world, gave him the phone number of the flat in

Wimpole Mews. It was a bad move, for Gordon was never off the phone. He called Keeler his girl to friends and pestered her. She even moved in with him for a while but, realizing it would not work, moved out again. Gordon became so obsessed with her that he would not leave her alone.

In mid 1962 Keeler met another West Indian, John Edgecombe, handsome and in his late twenties. She appealed to him for help which was another unwise move and was to bring disaster upon disaster, because her contact with him was an integral part of the snowball once it began to roll.

Edgecombe gave her the help she needed; he took her in and they lived together for a while before she flitted back to Ward again. But the damage had been done. The two West Indians knew about each other; both wanted her and both were jealous of each other. Both were virulent and sometimes violent men. Both came from a culture where once a girl belongs to a man he insists that she stays that way. They were, however, dealing with a girl who spread her friendship and favours around and they could not understand it.

As time went on Gordon and Edgecombe heard about her affair with the British minister, Profumo. That in itself did not matter because it was hearsay and who was going to believe the word of a black man from Notting Hill against that of a senior Tory and a minister of the Crown. No paper was going to touch that with a bargepole unless there was proof.

Two months after Ward had started down the short slope to real depravity, he took his two prodigies, Keeler and Rice-Davies, to a party given by a very well-known hostess – Mariella Novotny, Yorkshire born and only twenty. Her parties were so erotic that she was sometimes known as the government chief whip for as well as coupling, tripling and sex in even greater numbers, flagellation was part of the entertainment.

It was all very jolly and everyone enjoyed it a great deal, for much of the thrashing was for stimulation or for the sake of trying something different to see if it was worth pursuing. This was in the days when everyone knew about public school canings and beatings, a subject about which many spoke and many wrote, and one that was not underground as it is today. This was the start of the civilized society, as many were to call it, following on from the more starchy post-war forties and fifties.

On the night that Ward, Keeler and Rice-Davies arrived at

the party in Hyde Park Square the main orgy of the evening was over. Guests were exhausted and many were lying naked on sofas and beds, some with their bottoms well marked, others just fornicating away happily. The hostess (who was to die in 1983 from inhalation of vomit mixed with an overdose after toppling face first into a jelly) was on a bed entertaining six men at once. It was no more than one would expect of a hostess who sometimes served badger as the main dish but on this occasion had laid a pair of peacocks before her guests while her rich and beaming and much older husband proudly looked on.

Ward's girls were really shocked. Ward told them many prominent people were there – judges, MPs and stars from the cinema and theatre. (Two years later, at the height of the Affair, Macmillan said that he had been told that there had been thirteen judges at an orgy in Belgravia the night before. He wiped a world-weary hand across his brow and said: 'Five I could believe, but not thirteen'.) However there is no doubt there were guests at that party who would not have liked it known that they were there and among them was one who became famous when the Affair broke nearly two years later.

This was the Man in the Mask and his identity was a subject that puzzled Lord Denning greatly and took up much of his time when he held his inquiry later. There were rumours that he was a Cabinet minister, that he was this minister, that he was that MP, or that senior Tory who everyone knew loved to have his arse tanned as if he was a fag at Eton again, or that young up-and-coming Tory who loved such parties.

The truth, as Denning discovered, was much less exciting. The Man in the Mask was a masochist who had money, was in business and enjoyed being the object of public humiliation to a certain extent. He covered his face with a rubber mask so that only those who knew him very well or knew his anatomy could identify him.

For Mariella's peacock party he was strapped between two wooden pillars in the hall, and on a table to his side lay a whip. Each guest as he or she arrived was invited to give him one lash of the whip which they did with relish and he relished it in turn.

So 1961 ended. The state of play was purely individual. As we have seen, there were strands, spokes going out from an imaginary hub, but there was no hub, no pattern because there was nothing at the centre.

There was Ward with his girls. Rice-Davies was with Peter Rachman. Keeler was with Ward, but was being pursued by her West Indian friend Lucky Gordon – who was to be very unlucky.

Ward was mixing in Russian circles with Ivanov and being watched by MI5 and illegally by MI6, who were supposed to operate only outside the country. The Foreign Office and the Home Secretary did not know this but the Foreign Office knew what Ward was about because he had made no secret of it.

Profumo was back with his wife, his dalliance of four months ago long finished. Apart from the 'Darling' letter, and in his circles everyone was darling, there was nothing to link him with Keeler except her word and who was going to take that; in any case, why should she talk? Time was a great healer.

Wigg was still smarting over Kuwait and what he was hearing. He knew nothing of Profumo and Keeler and in ordinary circumstances if he had heard of a minister sleeping with a pretty girl he would have done nothing about it. It was none of his business.

And there was John Lewis. At this stage he knew nothing, not a thing.

11

1962

1962 started badly for Lewis. His company was still in big trouble when he went to the Court of Appeal in March. There was a drop off in trade and orders. The legal cast was the same, appearing this time before three judges, but no jury. The appeal by the two newspapers was based on the extensive damages and on the issue of innuendo – what the articles would have meant to ordinary people. After a great deal of legal argument over that point, the judges reserved their judgment, which they finally gave on 4 April 1962.

They said that the legal point on innuendo had been left to the jury by the judge (against whom there was no criticism) without direction that the words were not capable of bearing the imputation that fraud had been committed. The matter of innuendo should not have been given to the jury to consider, but should have been withdrawn by the judge.

On damages the judges all agreed. They thought they were not only unreasonable but were out of all proportion to the sum which could properly be found on the evidence. Lord Justice Holdroyd Pearce said that he could not help feeling that the case had become somewhat divorced from reality. No indication of financial damage was given in the main evidence.

It had been suggested, he said, that the jury might draw the most sinister inference from the fact that the papers had obtained information that they should not have had from the police, but had not disclosed the source. But because Lewis said that the inquiry had never started and the papers were not responsible for the police force, they were not liable for damages caused by the dilatory conduct, if any, of the police. It was clear that the second jury was influenced by the first.

Another of the judges said the damages were so large that no reasonable jury could have given them without taking into account something which they were bound to exclude from their considerations, the innuendo, which had to be proved and which could not be by mere imputation – and that the damages were out of all proportion to the facts of the case.

The judges, one of whom was Mr Justice Havers, father of the late Lord Chancellor Michael, and his sister Mrs Justice Butler-Sloss and grandfather of actor Nigel, allowed the appeal with costs and ordered a retrial.

Lewis promptly appealed to the House of Lords, the highest court in the land. But he was despondent. The money he had so hoped would be available to save his substantial company was not there. It would be months before the case was heard in the Lords. He took the only course possible. His company asked Lloyds Bank to appoint a receiver. In a statement Lewis, who was chairman and managing director, said;

> Had the company received the sum awarded by way of damages, it would have been able to finance the purchases of its raw materials for a further period which it is believed would have afforded it an opportunity of again making profits.
>
> However, since it became known that these matters were subject to further appeals, intense pressure has been put on the company by its creditors, as a result of which the company finds itself in difficulties. Accordingly it deemed it to be its duty to inform Lloyds Bank Ltd of the position and they have been invited to appoint a receiver in accordance with the terms of their debenture.

Rubber Improvement had reported losses for the previous three trading periods and on the day of the statement their two-shilling (10p) shares were down 3d to one-shilling and ninepence. It was the end of the family company and meant the loss of hundreds of jobs in Hayes and the east Midlands. It had been a good company, but times had changed.

Lewis spent a miserable time seeing the finish of all he had built up in the business world. He was still out and about, clubbing, meeting girls, seeing friends, still on the social round, listening to the gossip, feeding in what he heard and keeping his eyes and ears open for something that could put him in the good books of the Labour party leadership. He also listened out for anything which could do Ward harm, and it is certain that he would have made an anonymous call or two to some authority, putting the poison in for his enemy who, not that Lewis knew it, was making a name for himself with the security forces, although they were highly suspicious of him. But Ward was never anything other than a patriot, working for Britain even if pro-Russia, in an attempt to bring the two countries together. He and Ivanov were almost inseparable, Ivanov beavering his way into the social set to do his work for the motherland. The highlight of the first half of the year was when Ward took the Russian to Lord Astor's Ascot Week house party, which must have made his communist heart bleed with envy.

Two things occurred in July: Profumo threatened to resign over the decision to scrap the Blue Water missile project, one of many such projects that went on the heap during the sixties and seventies. He went to see Macmillan to protest at the decision and was almost in tears (Macmillan referred to him as 'the poor boy'), but the scrapping went ahead and Profumo did not resign.

In the same week *Queen* magazine, in its issue of 31 July, ran its regular column 'Sentences I'd like to hear the end of ', collected by the associate editor Robin Douglas-Home, nephew of the Foreign Secretary and later Prime Minister Lord Home, and a member of the royal set at the time. His ear was as close to the ground in the social round in London as anyone's. The innocuous sentence read: '... called in MI5 because every time the chauffeur-driven Zis drew up at her front door, out of the back door into a chauffeur-driven Humber slipped ...'

It was true in most details because for a very short time in the summer of 1961 (and, remember, this was over a year after Profumo had met Keeler) the paths of the British Cabinet minister and the Russian Naval attaché must have crossed, or nearly crossed in Ward's flat. The Russian mostly drove himself in his Zis to Wimpole Mews and Profumo did the same, not in an official Humber but in his Mini. Because Douglas-Home is dead it is not possible to find out who in the Chelsea set (the name for the swinging crowd that summer) told him. Alternatively it may have been someone from another group, such as Ward himself, for he could never keep his mouth shut and loved to shock with his revelations. The laws of libel stopped the magazine from going any further in naming names, but there were several who would have known to whom he referred and many others who would ask their friends. They may well have been given the answer, and smiled and left it at that. It is certain that Lewis saw or heard of the sentence and asked, like everyone else, who it referred to. He had at that time no idea that his great enemy had most of his fingers in the pie.

In the autumn, while Keeler was living with Edgecombe, much more important events were building up, leading to the brink of a nuclear holocaust. From 16 October to 27 October the Americans, led by Kennedy, and Russia, led by Khrushchev, flexed their mighty muscles over the Russians' determination to put missiles on Cuba and America's equal determination to make sure they did not. Neither was prepared to back off for days, and during that time there was a sense of real terror around the world. In these days with the Soviet Union broken up in freedom and the Iron Curtain lifted, it is hard to recall just how terrified people were. Everyone hoped that commonsense would prevail, that one side would back off, but neither would. Those who slept soundly were the rare ones. For most it was a case of listening to the radio every hour, watching every television programme, devouring every newspaper for hopeful signs and waiting. There was no panic, just a stomach-churning, wet-palmed acceptance of what could happen, what the result would be. Nevil Shute's *On the Beach* was far too real to bring comfort.

Britain was on the edge of the crisis (although William Vassall, the homosexual whom the Russians blackmailed to give them secrets, was gaoled for eighteen years in the middle of it on 22 October, giving rise to an inquiry which caused the biggest ever division between the press and government) with Lord Home keeping a watching brief. Into the cauldron stepped a saviour in the unlikely form of Dr Ward. He did have a point. His friend Ivanov came up with the idea, undoubtedly fed to him by Moscow, that Britain should mediate to resolve the conflict. America knew from photographs that sites were being prepared for middle-range ballistic missiles and later, further photographs showed that Russian ships loaded with nuclear missiles were heading for Cuba. The American Navy began to blockade Cuba as the Russian ships sailed on towards the island, and conflagration and a possible Third World War.

Ward's mission was to get Ivanov's message to the Foreign

Office that Britain should arrange a summit and bring an end to the crisis. The Russian's line, coming straight from the Kremlin, was that as neither the Russians nor the Americans would back off, it was up to the British to get the sides together and allow the Russians, who of course did not want war, to back out without loss of face. If the British used their influence (and who could do it better than Macmillan and Lord Home?) they could fix an immediate summit in London where the whole matter could be sorted out. All the while, the Russians sailed on and the Americans prepared not only to stop the ships but to mount an invasion on Cuba.

Ward asked for and obtained the help of his friend Sir Godfrey Nicholson who enlisted his friends at the Foreign Office. Ward also got Bill Astor to talk to his friend Lord 'Boofy' Arran, an eccentric but clever peer who had a great relish for life and fun and knew all the right people. Arran met Ivanov and heard what he had to say. He considered that it was a Russian ploy to drive a wedge between the allies and said so to the Foreign Office. It was the Foreign Secretary's view too. He said that it was a classic Russian manoeuvre to separate them, test their resolve and try to boost British vanity by suggesting that they organize the peace-saving conference.

Lord Home, who was on 'Dear Boofy', 'Dear Alec' terms with his old friend, made the British position clear to the Russian charge d'affaires, whom he summoned to the Foreign Office. He told him that Britain would stand by the Anglo-American accord and there would be no negotiations.

Ivanov was angry that his attempts to save the crisis had failed. He talked of how quickly Russia could destroy Britain, how a giant wave, created miles out to sea by a giant explosion, could smash New York.

When night fell on Saturday 27 October, people in Britain did not know what they would wake up to. The clash point was on Sunday. It could be the day the world ended, or there could be a change of heart. The churches were full that Sunday morning as people in their mortal terror turned to God as a means of salvation. It was no mass hysteria, just a nation that had seen it all before when the Nazis tried to crush them.

What effect it had is impossible to say, but late on Sunday commonsense prevailed and both the Russian and American leaders suddenly realized what they were doing. The Russian ships turned back and the American Navy retreated to base. It was all over and people everywhere slept easily; after that one action, relations between the two superpowers gradually improved over the years.

Ironically, Ivanov was dining at the decadent dinner table of Lord Astor at Cliveden when the news came through. He was very angry indeed and went on and on about it. He became a bore in the end. He ranted at Lord Arran, who had acted as his intermediary and to whom Ivanov had insisted that the British aristocracy was the key to the top, thus underlining the point that he was in Britain to worm his way into circles where he could cause trouble, and at Lord Longford. They were both thoroughly embarrassed and fed up with his moaning that he could not believe it, that it was a humiliation that Khrushchev would not take, and that there would be a strong reaction in Russia.

Ivanov was wrong. He was not to go to Cliveden again, but his friendship with Ward continued. Ward himself was delighted with the part he had played. He regarded himself as an honest broker who had done his best to help save mankind. He wanted to tell others outside his immediate circle and the Foreign Office, who did not regard his efforts as anything more than a fleabite, what he had done. So he wrote to Harold Wilson, then one of the leaders of the Labour party, to tell him his views on the Cuba crisis and how he had been an intermediary in the attempts between Russia and Britain to solve it. Wilson filed the letter and forgot it until some eight months later.

On the night that the Cuba crisis was called off, one of the sideshows that were eventually to become part of the main attraction when the Affair broke into the open, occurred in a seedy little club in Soho. In those days Soho was the centre for sex and strip shows, for clubs where drinks were expensive and girls for hire always on hand, for prostitutes who plied their trade in small rooms in the maze of alleyways where a man could find whatever relief he needed for a price. Already the clubs were beginning to get a haze of cannabis as well as cigar and cigarette smoke.

On that Sunday night Keeler was there with Edgecombe. Among the others drinking and talking under the cover of loud juke-box music was Gordon, and he was as jealous as hell. He approached the couple and there was an argument over whose girl she was, a razor appeared in someone's hand and unlucky Gordon got a slash across the cheek which needed seventeen stitches. There was much screaming and shouting and a lot of blood. Gordon was hurried out and to hospital. Edgecombe was escorted away and although there was talk of charges, nothing happened because Keeler was not prepared to press them, and did not want the police involved. Edgecombe denied cutting Gordon and was later acquitted of the charge.

Lewis heard about it. He did not frequent that particular club but he learned of a fight and that the girl concerned was called Christine Keeler. He knew who she was by name, but was not sure whether he knew her by sight. He did not think so, because there were many girls like Keeler around the clubs, either working or escorting men friends. He was right. He did not know her, but he had had a whisper that she was the girl who had slept with Profumo. There was no proof, just a word, a nod and wink on the circuit on which he travelled. He made more inquiries, asking discreet questions and gaining information.

His inquiries ran parallel with the row that was brewing between the government and the press over Vassall. It was to become a witch-hunt by some newspapers, which accused the Civil Lord, Thomas Galbraith, of being too friendly with Vassall while he was working at the Admiralty after coming back from Russia, where he had been compromised by KGB – taken pictures of nude sexual activity with other men into spying.

The charges were totally untrue and Galbraith was cleared by the tribunal that Macmillan set up. But Galbraith later resigned, unable to accept Macmillan's advice that he should stay because he had done nothing. Macmillan accepted the resignation which came at a time when Profumo's troubles were beginning to bubble, and it may have been the Galbraith experience which stopped the Prime Minister from seeing Profumo. When the tribunal sat a nasty rift was created between the press and the government which worsened when two reporters were gaoled, in an act without precedent, for failing to reveal their sources.

Wigg was keeping an eye on the Vassall case and its ramifications, as he kept his eye on anything military or involving security, but he was more concerned with the Kuwait fast-force operation which had happened fifteen months earlier (yet another example of how slowly everything moved in this story). A senior doctor in the Royal Army Medical Corps had produced a report which showed that if there had been any fighting in the campaign the British soldiers would have been in serious trouble and there would have been very heavy casualties because of heat exhaustion. The men were not prepared for such heat as they found in the desert (unlike the 1991 Gulf War, there was no time to become acclimatized), and as many as ten per cent were out of action within five days of arriving, without any fighting at all. The report said that extensive tests had been carried out which showed that without a full week of acclimatization before fighting, the troops would be dangerously vulnerable to heat exhaustion. That was not all. Officers had mistakenly restricted water supplies when they should have increased them, and much of the clothing and equipment had been unsuitable.

Stories began to appear in the papers and Wigg, who was meticulously fair, was worried that the Secretary of State for War, whom he still liked and admired, would mistakenly think that he was responsible for planting them, which he was not. Wigg decided to take action and went to see Profumo's under-secretary to say he had not been responsible for the stories in the papers. Then he saw Profumo himself and they discussed a way by which Wigg could raise his misgivings about the Kuwait operation in the House of Commons during a general debate on the Army and the RAF which had been fixed for 23 November. Wigg was pleased. Profumo was behaving in the way he expected. The plan was for Wigg to speak first, and then Profumo would speak later. This procedural form of debate meant that Wigg would not get a chance to speak again, but he was not worried about that. He took Profumo at his word.

Wigg prepared his speech carefully. He had all the facts. He needed to marshal them so that they were right, and so that the Secretary of State could answer them as they had agreed.

Twelve days before the debate, Wigg went to his Dudley constituency for the annual Armistice Day service. After the service in Stourbridge, he accepted an invitation to lunch at the home of his agent, Councillor Tommy Friend, and when they reached the house he was told there had been a phone message for him. He naturally assumed it came from his wife, the only person who knew where he was, and he rang her at home. She said she had not called him. Wigg was puzzled. No-one knew he was there, he was sure of that. A little while later there was another call to his agent's home. It was a muffled voice and when Wigg took the receiver it said: 'Forget about the Vassall case. You want to look at Profumo.'

It was difficult to tell whether it was a man or woman, so disguised was the voice. The message made no sense at all. Why look at Profumo? Wigg wondered. He was already looking at Profumo. He was helping him to expose the cock-up of the Kuwait operation, not to cause trouble but to make sure it never happened again. So what could it mean? Who had made the call? It must be someone who knew him well, he reasoned. Someone who would be able to track him down. It would be someone who knew others in the Labour party very well, as they would know that Wigg always went to his constituency for Armistice Day, and would be there with his agent, who was also a good personal friend. It must be someone to whom he talked, but not someone with whom he moved every day; not a close colleague, because there would then be no point in resorting to subterfuge. So who? It was in fact John Lewis, although Wigg did not know this at the time nor was he ever to know it, because Lewis did not tell him. So why did Lewis ring Wigg?

In the days following the slashing, Lewis had been asking around for every piece of information he could gather about the girl and Profumo. He asked in the right circles, for he was told about Ivanov as well. The rumour had swelled and swelled in the immediate circle of those who knew, and had become almost a tale of musical beds. Lewis put it together in his astute mind and saw that there was capital to be made if he acted swiftly and strongly. He did not have enough information to go see his old racing friend George Wigg and tell him outright but he had enough to make an anonymous phone call which could be followed up when he had more, when he could confirm the story that the British minister and the Russian embassy man were sharing the same girl. Was not that a risk to security? Lewis could see himself being gratefully thanked for his services and perhaps some job with the party would come his way, which could lead to greater things. It was no trouble to find Wigg. Lewis knew he went to his constituency regularly at weekends, that the old soldier would be at the service, that it was more than likely he would be at his agent's home. A call to direct enquiries did the rest.

As Lewis celebrated, as Wigg pondered, Keeler bought a gun for £25 from a friend to protect herself. It was taken off her by her then lover Edgecombe, who said she should not have such a weapon – it was foolish.

On 23 November Wigg stood in the House of Commons and made his case over Kuwait, calling for an enquiry into the operation and the things that had gone wrong. When he sat down he discovered other things had gone wrong, for it was the Air Minister who rose and said that the faults had been grossly exaggerated and where there had been faults they had all been put right. A deep frown appeared on Wigg's face.

Then the balding smooth Profumo rose and began to speak. Wigg quickly realized that the Secretary of State was not sticking to the script. He did not refer to the report from the doctor, but mentioned two letters criticising Wigg for things he had not said in a newspaper article. Wigg was livid because Profumo had rung him the night before to discuss what was going to be said. Wigg considered that what Profumo was doing on such a serious problem was irresponsible, playing politics. Profumo went on and on, ignoring what they had planned, claiming that the surprise was that so much had gone right. Wigg could do nothing but take it. He knew because of the agreement he had with Profumo that he could not speak a second time, could not get up and say that Profumo was not saying what he should. Profumo has never commented on the allegation and refuses to do so.

Wigg was to say later that he had been trussed up and done and humiliated in public. He was a man with a very long memory. He was prepared to wait his time and strike when given the opportunity.

It was a bad mistake on Profumo's part. It may be that he thought he was doing nothing other than being a Tory against a Socialist, but he did not fully appreciate Wigg's passion for the Army. It was his first love. He was in the tank corps as an ordinary soldier from 1919 until 1937 and then commissioned, rising to colonel as he served right through the Second World War.

So, though he did not know it, Lewis had a much better ally than he thought when he made the call on Armistice Day. He read the reports of the debate and could see that the Tories had made rings round his racing friend. What he did not know was that the script, so carefully rehearsed by the two old soldiers, had been abandoned by a man who had told a Russian Naval officer that he should never trust a minister of the Crown.

By the end of November, fifteen months after Profumo had

broken with Keeler, leaving her with three letters (only one of which she retained) MI5 and MI6 were still watching the Russian and knew nothing of the girl with whom both men had slept. Lewis had sown a seed with Wigg, hoping for good things for himself, but having no idea Ward was involved. Wigg was making discreet inquiries about why he should drop his investigations into Vassall, about which he was none too happy, and look at Profumo. What could it mean?

Then three more ingredients were thrown in. On 29 November Rachman died of a heart attack at the age of forty-two and a heart-broken and potentially suicidal Mandy Rice-Davies moved back with Ward.

In the first week in December, Lewis's appeal against the court of appeal's ruling that there should be a retrial in his libel action against the *Daily Mail* and the *Daily Telegraph* began.

It was the same line-up of the bar, except that Neville Faulks, QC, had been promoted to the bench, before four Law Lords. They listened to the arguments over the meaning of innuendo, and what the ordinary man would infer from the article about the activities of the Fraud Squad, and the factual point on the size of damages. Then they reserved judgment, but did not fix a date. Lewis left the court still not knowing whether he would get any damages or not and with the frightening prospect that he might have to pay the mounting costs, which were already well into thousands of pounds. He knew that it was too late anyway to save the company. That would go under – and did – within the next few months. It was a miserable ending to what had been a success story.

The third and final ingredient was that just a few days later, Edgecombe turned up with a loaded gun.

12

THE SHOOTING

About 1 p.m. on Friday 14 December 1962, Johnny Edgecombe arrived outside Ward's home in Wimpole Mews in a minicab. He had come to get his girl back. She was inside, but would not have been if Rice-Davies had not taken so long doing her hair for their trip out. It was lucky they were still in the flat.

For Edgecombe had the gun, the one Keeler had bought for £25 with ammunition for her own protection a few weeks earlier. She was worried about her other West Indian lover, Lucky Gordon, who had had his stitches out and had taken them round to Ward and given them to him with a word of warning for the girl.

When Rachman died, Rice-Davies was genuinely distraught and even took an overdose, being found just in time by Keeler and one of her girl friends. So Keeler left Edgecombe and went to cheer up her friend. This did not suit him at all. He phoned but she told him to leave her alone. She was fed up with the West Indian sex and drugs scene, and wanted to go back to a normal life.

Edgecombe would not listen. Suddenly he was on the doorstep in this quiet and attractive central London mews with a shooter. In 1962 guns were almost unheard of, certainly in that residential part of London. But Edgecombe had one and when Rice-Davies went to the window she told him that Keeler was at the hairdresser.

Her story might have worked, except for the way she kept turning back into the room to ask Keeler what she should say next. Edgecombe immediately realized that she was there, so she went to the window and told him to go away. She asked him if he had a gun and he said no, but when she went to phone the

Mandy Rice-Davies and Christine Keeler at the height of the scandal. They shared much in common, including, Peter Rachman

Lucky Gordon, outside Marylebone Court in October 1963, who was wrongly accused of attacking Christine Keeler and her ex-lover

The prosecutor, Mervyn Griffith-Jones, in the Ward trial. He spoke in olde worlde English and regarded Ward as a thoroughly filthy fellow

James Burge, the man who had the uphill task of defending
Stephen Ward

The Russian naval attaché,
Captain Eugene Ivanov, who
spied for his Motherland
and shared a bed with
Keeler at the same time as
the Minister for War

Stephen Ward leaving the Old Bailey, quite cheerful after a day of prosecution evidence which was not as bad as he had feared

Mandy Rice-Davies on a high in December 1963

George Wigg becomes
Paymaster-General in
October 1964 when Labour
wins the election – the fall-
out of John Lewis's hatred
for Ward

Lord 'Bill' Astor, Ward's great friend – until the police began
investigating, armed with Lewis's dossier

Profumo arrives home after confessing to his wife. The next morning he resigned, a ruined man, after telling Macmillan and his colleagues that he had lied

Lord Denning about to start
on his report

Stephen Ward arriving at the Old Bailey on 29 July, just two days
before he took the overdose that killed him

Lewis in the sixties at the time of his great triumph – *fixing* Ward

(*below*) Macmillan with his wife

police he started shooting at the door lock. When she went to the window again a bullet thudded into the woodwork beside her.

As the police, followed by the press who had been tipped off by friends in the neighbourhood, roared with sirens blaring, to the mews, the girls cowered under a bed and the gunman fled, hurling his gun into the garden behind the house.

Police worked out that he had first tried to charge the front door and when that did not work he fired into the lock. It took three shots before it gave way, but the window was opened at that moment and he shot once or twice and then ran out of ammunition. He then got back into the minicab and was driven back to Brentford in west London where he was arrested and charged with the shooting and also with slashing Gordon on 27 October.

The girls were taken to the police station to be questioned and Keeler rang Ward. He was not amused. He might have gone downmarket, but he still had his patients and rich friends to think about, for whom he was a focal point for pretty girls. 'Food from Fortnum and Mason, drink from Justerini and Brook, and girls from Stephen Ward' was the joke the next summer when it all became very serious. He did not relish the thought of them knowing that two black men were fighting over his little baby who had also gone downmarket. He told both girls to get out.

The papers loved it: black men fighting over a girl who mixed in the top circles, a well-known host and osteopath, an artist who sketched portraits of royalty and politicians, the hint of drugs and knifes, low life in Notting Hill, high life in Cliveden. At that point no-one knew about Profumo and because of the size of Lewis's damages against the papers, no-one would have gone near him, even if they had known.

But the shooting opened Keeler's mouth and her tongue would not stay still. On the night of the shooting she met a friend who had given her advice, a retired solicitor called Michael Eddowes. He had written a book about the miscarriage of justice over Timothy Evans in the case of the 10 Rillington Place mass murders by John Christie, and was to become one of the greatest experts in the world on the Kennedy murder in November 1963. It was to him that she poured out her story, telling him about the men she had slept with, including Ivanov –

whom Eddowes had met and argued with over Russia's intentions during the Cuban crisis – and various other details.

Eddowes did nothing with the information except write an 1,800 word memo which he was to send to the Prime Minister three months later when matters began to boil. He also told his friend, the Danish consul, but Eddowes's view was that the security forces must have been watching what was going on and would know everything that Keeler had told him. He was right that they were watching what was going on, but he was not to know that they knew nothing of the sex. When they did they still did nothing about it because they considered that the morals of a minister, provided they did not affect security, were none of their business.

Nine days after the shooting, with Edgecombe remanded in custody and Gordon out of sight, Keeler went to a Christmas party at Rossmore Court, Marylebone. It had been organized so that old friends from the Cabaret Club could get together. It was a friendly occasion and everyone was in festive spirit. Among the guests was a pleasant man, in his late forties, fattening a bit, average height, balding but interesting to talk to and a good listener. It was Lewis.

All the talk was about the shooting because what had happened was common knowledge either from the papers or from the gossip in the clubs and pubs. Everyone wanted to hear Christine's side of it.

Everything would have been all right if she had just stuck to what had happened at the flat. But for the first time she had found a friendly shoulder to cry on and she wanted to tell all. She could not have known that the shoulder belonged to a man who was not the friendly fellow he appeared, but Ward's sworn enemy, an enemy determined to destroy Ward.

At first, as others moved away, having heard enough of what she had been up to, she again recounted the shooting and her friendship with the two coloured men. She told how she had been lovers of both and how they were jealous and fought over her, how Gordon and Edgecombe had attacked her.

Lewis, still low after the inconclusive appeal, pushed her onwards, filling her glass, giving her a cigarette and lighting it. Then she began to talk about her other lovers and friends – a Russian, Jack Profumo, Bill Astor, Stephen.

'Stephen who?' asked Lewis, who had told her that he

understood her plight because he had been libelled by two papers and had had to sue.

'Ward,' said Keeler. A four-letter word, a name, no more than that to the average person, just a four-letter name. As she spoke it she had no idea what she was saying. How could she?

But in that second she sealed the fate of the government. From then on, what had been a brief affair, a bit of a laugh because she was sharing a Russian spy and the Tory War Minister, a bit of gossip, became a major scandal that will be notorious until the end of time. Every history book to be written about Britain in the future will mention it, sometimes in a chapter, sometimes in a paragraph, but it will always be remembered because a twenty-year-old girl met an embittered politician who was trying to get back into favour and who loathed the man she had just named with an intensity that passes most human understanding.

What has he to do with it, Lewis wondered. He gave her no hint of what she had just done. He must have been beside himself with delight. His adrenalin must have been flowing; he must have felt as if he had drunk the finest champagne and was on a wonderful high that could only get better. No Christmas present could ever beat the one she had just given him, not even the massive damages awarded him for a libel exactly four years before. His brain must have crashed with the sheer thrill of working out the combinations of what he could do with this information, and he still had not heard it all. He could go to Wigg with real information, not a muffled voice down the phone anonymously, he could go to the police with facts, not anonymous letters, and to the inland revenue and to the … the variations were endless. This was wonderful, this was the magical music he had waited for ten years to hear. This would fix Stephen Ward once and for all. He carried on listening.

Keeler told him the lot – how Ward found her, how he shaped her the way he wanted her (Eliza Doolittle? Trilby? take your pick), who she had slept with, how she had met famous people at Cliveden and at Stephen's flat. She told how they had gone to orgies and wild parties, and how they had moved downhill, how Stephen had made her get drugs and black girls at low cafes in Paddington and Notting Hill.

Lewis asked her questions. The lovely girl kept talking. She had met one person who would help her in her troubles now that

Ward and Astor were deserting her, she said. He kept probing away as they sat slightly apart from the others and she told him everything, except for one fact which she kept back until later.

She told him more than enough. He told her that he could help her, that she must get a solicitor and he would arrange that after Christmas. She went off to celebrate Christmas thinking all was well, that she had an answer to her troubles and worries.

Lewis went back to his flat and sat down to think about what he had been told. He could not really believe it. He had been given two wonderful presents. First there was the ammunition to hit Ward and hit him very hard. He was obviously running some kind of call-girl racket just as Lewis had claimed all those years before, when it was not true. He was mixing with some very rum people and he clearly needed investigating on that score. Secondly, there was the security issue and that could be used in two ways, firstly to get back in with the Labour leadership, and secondly to fix Ward again as some kind of Russian sympathizer and possible spy.

But could Profumo have been so silly as to share a girl with a Russian Naval attaché who was clearly up to something nasty on the espionage front? Was this just the chatter of a girl whose tongue had been loosened? He would have to question her further to see if she stuck to the story, for it was not something that a girl would just make up. It would sound too far-fetched for that.

A few days after Christmas, Lewis invited Keeler round to his flat in St John's Wood and she went. She did not know that he taped their conversation. Lewis said he had found her a solicitor, because she would need to be represented in court when Edgecombe came up, since there was no doubt that he would attack her. He was facing a very long sentence. Possessing a gun and firing it in the street would alone carry a heavy penalty. Then he took her through her story again. He kept going back to Profumo, even though she insisted it was all over long ago, fifteen months ago, which was a long time in her life, and in most people's, that she did not want all that raked up because it was nothing to do with what was happening now. But Lewis was persuasive and she told him about the letters and how Ward had asked her to ask Jack when the Americans were going to give the Germans the bomb ...

'The what?'

'The nuclear bomb,' she said.

Lewis could not believe it, could not take in what she was saying. This was dynamite, this was more than he could have ever hoped for; who was this beautiful, wonderful person who was telling him everything he had always hoped he would hear?

He asked her to repeat it and she did.

Then, satisfied that he had every dot and tittle that she could provide, Lewis did what he normally did with a pretty girl. He made a pass at her. There was a scene where he threatened her, verbally at first, saying that everything about her past would come out in court and she could be locked up for perjury if she lied. Then it became physical. Keeler claims that he produced a gun and said that there was no way she could leave until they had had sex, and dramatically added that to get out she would have to shoot him first. She was astonished but took the gun, pointed it at him and pulled the trigger. He had told her it was loaded, but she did not know if it was. Lewis went white and staggered back. Luckily it was not loaded, but he kept saying, 'You could have shot me, you could have shot me.' He opened the door and she ran out. She did not see him again.

But Lewis had every word she said on tape. He had a story of an incredible security lapse that could do the Labour party only good. He had a story of girls for the rich and the man who provided them who sounded like a pimp living off immoral earnings who should be punished for it. The fact that it was Stephen Ward was a bonus that comes only once in a lifetime of hating.

Let us consider what would have happened if Lewis had not gone to that Christmas party and had not met Keeler.

Up to that stage there were rumours and very little more. Even if the press had had the guts to try to follow the rumours, and it is quite understandable that they were not going to risk the kind of sums that had been awarded to Lewis for what was a very minor story, what would they have to print? They would have had the word of a girl who was sharing favours with two West Indians. She was claiming an affair with a minister and a Russian embassy official. The reporters would go along and see Ward who was extremely angry about the black man shooting up his home in a respectable part of London and bringing him into disrepute, and had all but abandoned Keeler. He would want no part of it and would deny everything.

They would go to Profumo who would deny everything vehemently and say that he would sue if they printed anything. Ivanov would go to ground and leave the country, and Bill Astor would deny it all, as he was to in court. The reporters would sniff around and pick up some dirt from other Ward girls and go back to Profumo and he would get his solicitors, Theodore Goddard, one of the leading firms in the country, to write to the editor and tell him what would happen if they did not desist.

Perhaps word would have finally drifted back to the Whips' office in the House of Commons, and the Chief Whip might have had a word with Profumo about the tittle-tattle. Profumo could have played it one of two ways. He could have admitted it and said it was all over but if they felt he should resign because of, say, an operation he was to have which would make it hard for him to do his ministerial job properly for six months (until the gossip went away), that would be all right with him, as long as he could continue in office when he came back. Or he could have denied it. Either way it would have all been swept under the carpet with hardly any fuss at all.

But Lewis knew the truth, and he would never give up.

13

OUT IN THE OPEN

Sixteen months after Profumo had last slept with Christine Keeler, John Lewis rang his friend George Wigg and asked to see him. He had some important news to tell him.

Wigg, who had been pursuing the Vassall case with his usual vigour and occasionally wondering why he should look at Profumo, without much success because he had not heard the rumours, fixed a morning meeting on 2 January 1963 in his room in the House of Commons. He was not sure what he was going to hear, but he did not expect much. He agreed to see Lewis because he was an old parliamentary colleague, because he knew him from the racetracks and because he was always interested to hear new information.

Lewis arrived for the first meeting with enough information to make Wigg call for any more he could find. Lewis told how he had met 'a Miss Christine Keeler' at a party just before Christmas and that she was building a reputation as the most notorious woman in London. She had said that she had a friend, 'a Mr Stephen Ward', whom she had heard refer to Lewis, and had asked this Mr Ward if she could phone him (Lewis) because he could possibly befriend her. It was a deliciously light touch and a barefaced lie by Lewis, because he was not going to spoil the moment for which he had waited so long.

He told Wigg a story that was quite true, about the shooting, about Ward who had naked games of hide and seek with his guests at Lord Astor's estate at Cliveden, how Ward had influential friends and how this girl, this 'Miss Christine Keeler', claimed that she had slept with both the Secretary of State for War and a Russian Naval attaché who might well be heavily involved in espionage.

Wigg nearly fell off his chair. He asked Lewis to repeat it, which he gladly did. He said that he had met Keeler several times and had questioned her closely and had taken notes of what she had said. If Wigg was interested ... if Wigg was *interested* indeed! ... he would be prepared to bring these notes along to a subsequent meeting if Wigg felt one was necessary, because he (Lewis) thought these facts might be a matter of national security.

The colonel wrote everything down in longhand, relishing, no doubt, every fact but not nearly as much as the former colleague who was feeding them. Lewis kept his secret magnificently. Never once did he let on that he had known and hated and loathed Ward for many years and would do anything in his power to do him down. It was a long time before Wigg had an inkling about the past and how Lewis's vendetta was the real cause for the revelations.

Lewis was back the next day with more. Wigg, who had spent all day, evening and night thinking about what Lewis had told him and what he could do with it and what would be the best way of going about it, made tea and they talked on. It was then that Lewis let slip, acting like a good negotiator by giving his game out little piece by little piece, that Ward had made a specific request to the girl, this 'Miss Christine Keeler'. He has asked her, Lewis said, to ask Profumo about the supply of atomic weapons by the Americans to Germany while she was with him, either in the car or in bed.

Wigg stared at Lewis for some time. 'What?' he asked, and made him repeat it.

Lewis did. 'I felt the same when she told me,' he said. 'It's almost unbelievable. A minister, a defence minister at that, and a Russian spy sharing the same girl and she's been asked to ask the War Minister when the Americans are going to give the Germans nuclear warheads.' He shook his head in amazement.

Wigg pressed him further. Had the Russian asked her to get the information from Profumo? No, Lewis said, not as far as he knew. He had asked her about this and she had been vague for a moment, but had then said definitely not. She had also said, Lewis stressed, that she had never asked Profumo.

Wigg snorted. If this girl was blabbing like this to anyone she met (although Lewis had assured him that she was not), the security problem, and it was a major security problem, was going to grow.

He asked Lewis questions in the same way that Lewis had cross-examined Keeler. But this was quite different. Keeler wanted to tell all because she thought that her mentor was cross and was not going to support her any more, and once she had started there was not much anyone could do to shut her up. Lewis was cool and selective. He was only telling as much as he wanted Wigg to hear. He told him that his motive in bringing this to Wigg was his national duty to report that such a terrible breach of security had occurred so that something could be done about it.

Is the Russian still here? Wigg asked. Oh yes, Lewis assured him. Keeler had seen him a couple of days before with his friend, this Mr Ward.

Wigg thought quickly. He could not imagine that Profumo was a security risk. He could accept that he might have been fool enough to sleep with the girl because that was nothing unusual: pretty girls attracted middle-aged men with the seven-year itch and Profumo had been married seven years when he met Keeler. He knew colleagues, members of the government party, friends in the world outside parliament, who had girl-friends and mistresses, and so what? He might not approve but he certainly was not going to condemn. But even in the height of passion, and afterwards in the lull of satisfaction, the minister was not going to discuss what the Americans might or might not do with nuclear warheads and Germany even if he knew, which was very unlikely. He was not in the Cabinet and it was unlikely that he would have access to such information. Even if he did, he was far too astute and intelligent to do anything so silly as talk about it.

Wigg thought about going to Profumo direct and telling him what Lewis had told him. It was certain that Lewis did not know Profumo, he had indeed said so, but he had told Wigg that Profumo apparently did know Ward well and that Ivanov was in the circle. Neither Lewis nor Wigg knew, and how could they know, that the Cabinet Secretary had warned off Profumo sixteen months before this extraordinary conversation.

But if he went to Profumo direct, what would he do? Wigg no longer trusted him. The manner in which Profumo had stitched him up in the Kuwait debate two months earlier more than rankled. He did not trust the smooth-talking Tory minister any more. He asked a friend, giving only vague details, what he should do. The friend confirmed his own feelings that having been caught once he should not give Profumo a second chance. Wigg, always an honourable man, was still doubtful. He was still worrying about the Vassall affair. Then just a few days later Hugh Gaitskell, the Labour party leader, died at the young age of fifty-six from a mysterious virus. It was a tremendous blow to the party for his rating with the public was increasing.

Wigg was one of the main organizers of his friend Harold Wilson's leadership campaign against the ebullient George Brown, a brilliant politician for whom, sadly, one drink was one too many. On St Valentine's Day, 1963, Wilson won the second ballot by 144 votes to 103 and the new leader had no more faithful servant and watchdog than Wigg.

All the time this was going on Wigg was thinking what he should do about Keeler and Profumo, and the terrible security lapse that had occurred, according to Lewis. He was coming back with more and more information. He let Wigg have the tapes and they listened to them together. The more Wigg heard the more worried he became, because this was outrageous, even though it had all happened over sixteen months before. What to do? he kept asking himself.

Wigg had a friend in the highest ranks of the Metropolitan police, Commander Arthur Townsend, a fleshy stocky man, very experienced and now in charge of the department involving gambling, vice and licensing. At Wigg's suggestion, Lewis went to see him and talked at length, presumably giving him much of the detail that he had already given to Wigg. There would have been no point in not telling him everything because he had already set the snowball rolling, I say presumably, because there is no record of what happened and both Lewis and the commander are long dead. There is also no record of why nothing was done, but the reason for that may well be the fact that for many years Lewis had bombarded the Metropolitan police with complaints about incidents where he or a friend or member of the public had brushed with the law in a minor way, or had been offended by some police action. There was a thick file of his letters which were signed by him, and there was a file of other letters, anonymous but suspected as being from Lewis, including allegations against Ward.

When the letters came on House of Commons notepaper from Lewis as an MP they were acted on at once. In later years they were taken up only when the police knew the facts. Lewis was regarded as a nuisance, and it may well be that the commander, having heard him out, made some inquiries, found that no-one knew anything, and left it for the time being as yet another Lewis complaint.

It is certain that Lewis had a long conversation with the commander and kept the contact going over many months. Roy East, a very experienced journalist and on the *People* at the time, discovered just how close the contact was when Lewis took him to meet the commander about the Man in the Mask. Roy had met Lewis some weeks before, being put in touch with him by another Labour MP, Ben Parkin, following the strange murder, never solved, of a victualling supply officer at the Admiralty called Norman Edward Rickard, aged thirty-eight. Rickard was found naked, strangled, with his hands tied behind his back in a cupboard in Maida Vale, north London. A few days later another homosexual, Alan Vigar, aged twenty-three and a television studio wardrobe boy, was found dead in similar circumstances, except that he was in bed, in his flat in south London.

Roy said:

I met Lewis who knew all about the case. There was some talk at the time because of the Vassall tribunal that there had been orders from above to stop the investigation. From that initial meeting Lewis was on to me frequently and I got the impression that he wanted to know what was going on, for someone else. He was always pumping journalists for information. He was extremely smooth and suave, immaculately dressed, a bullshitter. He was condescending until you knew him well and then he was more down to earth. It was always 'dear boy' this and that whenever you met and I always thought he would make a perfect butler. He was a man who never gave his money away, a mean man.

Some time later when we were having coffee in a cafe near his home he asked me if I knew someone called Stephen Ward. I did. I met him in coffee bars and I liked him. He was amusing and charming without any pretence. He was no villain. Lewis was incensed with Ward, said he was going to fix him at any cost. He had this pathological hatred for Ward. I thought there was more to it than just his claim that Ward had slept with his wife. Both of them said there had been a bust-up about property but no-one ever got to the bottom of that.

What is certain is that Lewis was intense when talking about
Ward and almost lit up like a beacon so totally obsessed was he.
Ward always said that Lewis was an evil man who would do
anything to get his way, to get anyone, but particularly Ward. He
had no doubt that Lewis was not a man to be tackled. He did not
like Lewis and blamed him for all his troubles, although in the
later stages he blamed the government of the day. I saw him a
week before his trial and he blamed the government, saying that
he was a scapegoat, and he was very depressed. He was
convinced that the jury and judge had been nobbled and was
absolutely convinced that if he was acquitted something diabolical
would happen. He was convinced that he would be killed. I said
it was a load of twaddle. Who was going to do that? I asked in my
innocence.

That meeting came after Lewis took Roy to meet
Commander Townsend. Roy had had several scoops during the
Affair, including one concerned with identifying the Man in the
Mask at Mariella Novotney's party in 1961, as a Yorkshire
industrialist from Sheffield. Roy had found out from a retired
solicitor in Surrey who the man was and he mentioned it to
Lewis. By that time Roy considered Lewis a busybody but on
this occasion Lewis asked him if he would talk to a senior
Scotland Yard officer about it.
  Roy remembered:

I was given the red-carpet treatment when Lewis took me to
Scotland Yard. Townsend was a uniformed commander, a bit
under six foot with a slight stoop. He did not like the press. He
made that plain because he had had a run-in with somebody
from Fleet Street in the past. The drinks cupboard was open and
we talked. It was obvious that Townsend and Lewis knew each
other very well but not as friends.
  It was not surprising, because Lewis had been feeding
Townsend and the police with information since January and it
was now June.
  Townsend said he wanted to meet my informant about the
Man in the Mask and surprisingly my man agreed to meet
him on mutual territory and did so. Between Lewis and
Townsend there was a false courtesy. At the same time I felt they
did not trust each other and there was a coolness. At one stage
Lewis started talking about something, and I cannot remember
what it was, and Townsend's reaction was: 'I wish you had told

me that before.' Townsend clearly believed that Lewis knew a great deal more than he had told him at previous meetings.

A short time after that I had a call from Townsend to say they had seen the man in Yorkshire who had confirmed he was the Man in the Mask. Townsend asked me to meet him at pub near Scotland Yard and then took me off to lunch somewhere near Sloane Square.

I found out the real reason for the invitation when we sat down to eat. He asked me about Lewis because he was highly suspicious of him. I said that as far as I knew everything Lewis said seemed to be perfectly accurate but I regarded him as a busybody. Townsend wanted to know who Lewis was making inquiries for. Like me, he thought he was doing it for someone else but neither of us found out who it was, if someone did exist. Townsend said in passing, 'Of course you know that Lewis and Ward hate each other,' I had several meetings with Townsend after the Affair was over but he never said much more about Lewis.

Townsend had a high reputation among his colleagues for his fairness, his strict adherence to the rule of law and his courage. He won the BEM for his bravery in the Blitz in 1940. He was known as a man who was not flexible, never courted publicity and would give someone whom he thought was not receiving a fair deal his undivided attention.

Sir James Starritt, a former Assistant Commissioner who served with and under Commander Townsend, remembers: 'He was a great public servant. He stuck to the rules. If I was in trouble unfairly he would be the first man I would go to. If it was fair he would be the last. He had a great sense of fairness. He had great physical and moral courage. You always knew where you were with him. I would put my life on him, he was such a fair man.'

Lewis must have thought the same, because after his first meeting with the commander he went back to see him often. He also went back to Wigg time and time again with more information. Lewis had two great advantages: Ward did not know at the start that Lewis was behind Wigg and the public announcements of what had happened. Secondly, when Wigg discovered what was going on and that it was down to Lewis, Lewis already had spies in his camp, people who were in the crowds who drifted into Ward's flat and out again, journalists, friends, advisers, girls and more girls, people who were about town, people whom Lewis met and people whom Lewis asked specifically about Ward. For the next three months Lewis passed on what he knew either to Wigg or to his friend, Commander Townsend.

Lewis also gave Keeler another piece of advice, not directly but in a roundabout way. He suggested that a newspaper might be interested in her story, because it was all going to come out anyway. If it was true, she, as the central figure in a political and spying scandal was hot property. It was a clever move. Again he had stepped in first because he knew that although the papers would not dare touch a story about Profumo, even by innuendo, the reporters would dig and dig and might come up with something strong enough about Ward to print without trouble.

Keeler talked about it to her friends. They decided that her story was obviously worth money and that only two papers would be interested, the *Sunday Pictorial* (as the *Sunday Mirror* then was) and the *News of the World*. On the day that Ward was turnd out of his flat in Wimpole Mews because he could not pay the rent and had moved into Rachman's flat in Bryanston Mews, Keeler and Rice-Davies went to the *Pictorial*. Ward knew nothing about that and nothing about Keeler's meeting with Lewis, because he was not having anything to do with her. Even if she had told him about Lewis, it was too late. Everything was moving.

She sold her story to the *Pictorial* after the *News of the World* had refused to make a counterbid. The *Pictorial* offered her £1,000, £200 in advance and the rest when the story appeared. The publication of the 'Darling' letter was included in the deal. The other two letters had vanished or had been destroyed.

On 16 January a journalist went to see Ward and asked about the Edgecombe shooting. Ward said he knew a bit about it and told him. He also said that he hoped the whole thing would blow over. Ward talked to Ivanov about it and told him what he knew so far, which was by no means the whole story. Ivanov was much more attuned than Ward. He could see the political implications if things went the wrong way and knew that the enormous time-lag meant nothing in these matters. He discussed it with his masters in the Kremlin.

Keeler was by this time ensconced with the *Sunday Pictorial* reporters, who listened in amazement to what she had to say.

When she finally got round to saying that Ward had asked her to ask Profumo to tell her when Germany was going to get the bomb, they had the scoop of the year, if only they could print it.

This is the story that she gave them for their money:

Men are such fools. But I like them. I have always liked them.

Unfortunately, the combination of these things has led me into a lot of trouble and may even have risked the security of this country. It certainly could have been harmful to the country.

You see, one man who was foolish enough and irresponsible enough to have an affair with me was a cabinet minister, a member of Her Majesty's government.

And at the same time I was having an affair with another man – a Russian diplomat.

If that Russian or anyone else had placed a tape recorder or cine camera or both in some hidden place in my bedroom it would have been very embarrassing for the minister, to say the least.

In fact, it would have left him open to the worst possible kind of blackmail – the blackmail of a spy.

I am not suggesting that he really would have given up State secrets to avoid a scandal. He might have been tough and refused.

But I do believe that any man in his position – particularly a married man – is both unwise and irresponsible to have an affair with some unknown girl like me.

More especially so in this case because this minister had such knowledge of the military affairs of the western world that he would be one of the most valuable men in the world for the Russians to have had in their power.

He is, in fact, the Secretary of State for War, Mr John Profumo.

I believe now that a man in his position should not indulge in pastimes like me. I suppose even Cabinet ministers are only human, but I think they should curb their feelings when they take on the job.

One might think that as a politician he would have been particularly discreet in the affair. John Profumo was not. It is true he did not take me out much, but he did take me to his own home while his wife was away. And he did write letters to me.

One might also think that those responsible for State security would keep some sort of watch on men who hold as many secrets as he holds.

Yet if that happened he would never have been able to come

and see me at the flat where I was being visited by the Russian.

And believe me, the Russian was a man who would be very much aware of the value of the secrets which Profumo knew. He was not a civilian.

He was, in fact, a naval captain, Captain Eugene Ivanov.

Of course, at the time I did not realize the sinister implications behind my two affairs. I was only 18 and knew nothing of politics or international matters. I was not interested.

I did not realize then that blackmail is one of the Russians' favourite weapons when they are trying to recruit traitors or discover secret information.

I am sure that Jack Profumo would not have allowed his harmless affair with me to be used as a lever to prise secrets from him. But a weaker man in his position might have allowed it to happen.

At this time, however, I saw no danger in the situation. It just seemed funny to me that I should be seeing the two men, sometimes on the same day. One might leave my flat only a few minutes before the other arrived.

I did find it worrying when someone asked me to try to get from Profumo the answer to a certain question.

That question was: 'When, if ever, are the Americans going to give nuclear weapons to Germany?'

I am not prepared to say in public who asked me to find out the answer to that question. I am prepared to give it to the security officials. In fact, I believe now that I have a duty to do so.

Her account was never to appear in the paper and the *Sunday Pictorial*, which had the letter in the safe, did not use that either at the time, because of the libel laws. They would have to prove every word of it, which was impossible.

It was 8 February by the time Keeler had read every page of the story for the *Pictorial* and signed it as true. By that time, all hell had broken loose.

26 January was the day on which Lewis's plans came to fruition. Detective Sergeant Burrows went to see Keeler and Rice-Davies about the Edgecombe shooting. Later, he and Detective Chief Inspector Samuel Herbert were to be the two officers under Commander Townsend to investigate Ward and his girls to see if there was evidence that he had been living off immoral earnings or had committed any other sex-related offences involving prostitutes. On this occasion Burrows was interested only in the shooting, but he was to find two very angry

girls who were to feed Ward to the wolves, Keeler because she thought Ward had deserted her like, by then, Lewis, Profumo and Astor, and Rice-Davies because she was livid that Ward should have the flat in which her possessions were. When Rachman died she was heartbroken. She was also upset that he had left her nothing in his will and that she could not recover the gifts he had given her and her own possessions from Ward's flat.

The detective sergeant had not really gone to get a statement from either girl. He went only to warn them that they would have to give evidence in the Edgecombe trial. Keeler accepted that and then offered to make a statement. This is what she said and what he passed on to his superiors, who included Commander Townsend, in a memo:

She said that Doctor Ward was a procurer of women for gentlemen in high places and was sexually perverted: that he had a country cottage at Cliveden to which some of these women were taken to meet important men – the cottage was on the estate of Lord Astor; that he had introduced her to Mr John Profumo and that she had had an association with him; that Mr Profumo had written a number of letters to her on War Office notepaper and that she was still in possession of one of these letters which was being considered for publication in the *Sunday Pictorial* to whom she had sold her life story for £1,000. She also said that on one occasion when she was going to meet Mr Profumo, Ward had asked her to discover from him the date on which certain atomic secrets were to be handed to West Germany by the Americans, and that this was at the time of the Cuban crisis. She also said that she had been introduced by Ward to the naval attaché of the Soviet embassy and had met him on a number of occasions.

Two other things happened that day: Ward was told by a reporter that Keeler was with the *Sunday Pictorial* and telling all, and Lewis contacted the Special Branch and told them what he had already told Wigg, Commander Townsend and the Metropolitan police. He had dealt a potentially winning hand and waited to see how it would play before deciding whether to deal any more cards. He was later to tell the inland revenue, but that was just a repeat of his regular message to them that Ward was living off girls, and that his accounts as an osteopath and an artist showed that he was pocketing money without paying tax on it.

Ward went wild. He accused Keeler of trying to ruin his business by her activities, for his clients were hearing about what was going on and staying away in droves. Ward for them was an amusing chap, a good man to have around, an excellent osteopath, a gifted portrait artist and someone who could always lay on a few pretty girls for a party but ... and the 'but', which meant he was not quite one of them, was enough over the weeks that followed to make them quietly withdraw back into their own class. This was all part of the British hypocrisy which so fascinates and astonishes foreigners.

Ward decided to take action fast. He did not know that the police had a statement from Keeler which contained all the ingredients of what had happened sixteen months before, and that the detective sergeant had informed Special Branch. Keeler also told the police at Marylebone police station that she believed that Ward in a bid 'to have her put away', was going to allege that she was in possession of drugs. So the police decided that three officers, one from the Special Branch, one from the Metropolitan police and one from the Drug Squad, should go together to see Keeler and an appointment was made with her for 3.30 p.m. on Friday, 1 February 1963, at her flat in Great Cumberland Place in Marylebone.

The appointment was never kept by the police, and because it was not, the snowball increased its momentum. If they had visited her, the information that the girl would have provided in great detail – the layout of Profumo's house and bedroom – would have gone a very long way to proving her story and would have been passed to the Home Secretary or the head of MI5. Profumo could have been confronted with real ammunition instead of wishy-washy innuendo and rumour. He would have been in a position where he would have had to admit that he had had a short affair with Keeler.

But his luck held, although he did not know it. There was a breakdown in communications. Instead of all three going to see Keeler on 1 February no-one went near her again until 4 April. The Commander of the Special Branch had read the statement and decided that it would be better if his men did not go and see her, because if the press got to hear, as they undoubtedly would if Keeler started talking, it would cause a tremendous amount of speculation. He thought it would be better if the ordinary police went and reported back to Special Branch if there was anything they should know. So the appointment was cancelled and Keeler was rung and told it had been.

The reason why the Metropolitan police did not follow up the appointment was because the message had said that Ward should be seen, but there was no mention of Keeler. An appointment was made for Ward to come to the police station to see a drugs officer, but he never came. Knowing this, the police decided not to see Keeler again. It was a decision that was to lead to a great deal of trouble for many people.

As soon as Ward heard what Keeler was up to, he went to see Profumo and Astor on 27 January. They agreed on a plan of action to save their skins and their reputations, and acted together to try to stop what they saw as a potential disaster. Using their contacts, they learned that Keeler had told all to the *Sunday Pictorial* for £1,000 but their informants did not know exactly what 'all' was. They did not know that she had not yet signed the pages of her statement, which was essential before it could be printed (provided it got past the lawyers) and that the paper had put her up in a leading hotel in Albany Street, the normal practice of a newspaper that has someone under wraps.

They also learnt that the Edgecombe trial was to open on 5 February and that Keeler was the prime witness. She might blab names and Edgecombe might open his mouth too, and then the names would be out in public. Ward knew that Egdecombe, who had previous convictions, knew about Profumo and Ivanov and was dangerous: he might well talk if facing a long prison term. No-one knew what effect it would have. Would anyone believe them? It was unlikely but it was a risk.

Ivanov was another problem, but he acted on his own. The naval attaché, old Foxface as some knew him, vanished. He and his masters knew what would occur. They were old hands at this and they told Ivanov to come home.

The trio also found out that the *Sunday Pictorial* had the 'Darling' letter.

In the days before the trial there was tremendous activity to stop the dam that might well break with Keeler's story at the court. Her revelations could be terribly damaging to Astor, Ward and Profumo in ascending order. At the same time,

Profumo's colleagues heard the rumour and asked to see him to seek the truth. This is the timetable of what happened:

28 January 1963: Ward phoned Lord Astor and asked to meet him at the chambers of his counsel, William Rees-Davies, an MP, because he had a very urgent matter to discuss. That was an understatement. Ward quickly told Astor what was going on, and he went to brief his solicitor. Ward stayed to give Rees-Davies the gist of the story, saying that Keeler would name names, but not telling him of the real link.

That sent Rees-Davies to see the Solicitor-General, Peter (now Lord) Rawlinson, who told the Attorney-General, Sir John Hobson, formerly Profumo's head boy at Harrow, fellow undergraduate at Brasenose College, Oxford, and a fellow officer in the Northamptonshire Yeomanry. I mention this not to suggest that Hobson, an honourable man, would not do his duty properly, but because, having known Profumo over so many years, he would accept his word without question as an officer, minister and a gentleman.

Once he heard the rumour, Hobson sent Profumo a note asking him to come to see him, Rawlinson having told his senior colleague: 'Here is another of these rumours concerning another minister, Mr Profumo.' Hobson, just back from the Vassall tribunal where false rumours about another minister, Galbraith, were being examined, decided he would see his old friend Jack to see if he was going to sue, and whether he could help.

Before that meeting, Astor had been to see his solicitor and had then hurried round to tell Profumo of the danger.

Profumo acted at once and contacted Dick White, the head of the security services, and asked him to come round, which he did quickly. He brought with him Sir Roger Hollis, head of MI5. Both men knew Profumo had refused to take part in the honeytrap plot to turn Ivanov to British Intelligence. What Profumo was after was a 'D' notice, to gag the papers. This is a form of censorship the government can use when necessary to stop information damaging to the State being made public. It is rarely used. Hollis would not do what Profumo wanted. His view was that any security risk had ended when the minister stopped seeing Keeler in August 1961; and Ivanov, in any case, was going home.

Soon after this meeting, MI5 dropped all interest in Profumo and a directive was sent to all operatives that they were not to have anything to do with anyone involved. They were interested in security, not sex.

At eleven that night Profumo went to see Hobson at his home. As the two men sat over a whisky, Profumo began to dig his own grave and no man dug his own grave more thoroughly than the son of Baron Profumo. If he had told the truth, the matter might well have ended there and then. If Keeler had told all from the witness box, Profumo might have had to resign his office and go to the backbenches for a while on some spurious excuse before moving back into office again. People would have known he had had some kind of fling, but so what? But Profumo, despite a warning from Hobson that he must be absolutely frank otherwise he would not help him, denied the allegation that his conduct with the girl had been anything other than proper. It was this lie that set the snowball rolling faster and faster.

Hobson asked him questions. Profumo said he first met Keeler at Cliveden when his wife and many others were present. Subsequently he had met her with other guests at Ward's flat, twice when she was on her own for a short while before other guests had arrived. He had written her a short note beginning 'Darling', a meaningless term of endearment among show business people, to say he could not go to a cocktail party after being warned off by the security people when they discovered Ivanov was one of Ward's friends.

That was it, Profumo insisted, under his old friend's quiet cross-examination. No affair, no impropriety, no sex, no adultery. And, Profumo protested, he had now heard that on the basis of the association, the girl who had recently become a drug addict, and had been sleeping with two West Indians, was proposing to sell a false story to the newspapers which would ruin him.

Hobson replenished the glasses and told Profumo that if Keeler's story was true, he would have to resign. Profumo said there was no truth in it. Then, said Hobson, he would have to sue on publication of any such story and at once instruct the best solicitor possible. After Profumo left, Hobson sat thinking before phoning the Chief Whip, Martin Redmayne, to tell him what Profumo had said. Hobson was not happy; he remained slightly suspicious. But balanced against his suspicions was the word of his friend, and that he accepted.

29 January: Profumo went to see a partner in one of the leadings firms of solicitors, Theodore Goddard, and told the same story that he had given Hobson. It was not true.

Meanwhile, Ivanov was on his way to London Airport to end his tour of duty prematurely. He had been told by Ward what was going on and Ivanov and his masters were old hands at knowing when to leave the scene rapidly. He had done a good job, managing to gain entry to a group of important people, mixing with Ward and the Cliveden set, meeting ministers off duty and their friends. He had been allowed to put forward his views and to debate his corner. In hindsight his influence was minimal, although his masters still believed he had penetrated the true rulers of Britain, the aristocracy and Ivanov now claims his spying brought valuable information. But when Ivanov went he rightly suspected that, although his brief sharing of the same girl with a minister was over a year in the past, it might be resurrected for someone's personal or political motives.

30 January: Hobson discussed what Profumo had said with Rawlinson, and they decided they would go to have another chat with Profumo the next day. They accepted his story but ... Ward saw his counsel and talked tactics with Bill Astor, who was looking after himself without a solicitor.

31 January: Hobson and Rawlinson saw Profumo again. They asked if he would issue a writ for slander of libel if the occasion arose. Profumo said he most certainly would, even if it was against a friend or a colleague. What if the girl could prove it? they probed. Profumo said that he had not committed adultery, that not every man who was alone with a woman and called her darling was guilty of adultery. He said Keeler was quite a different person now from when he had known her in the summer of 1961; her manner and conduct had deteriorated and because of a few meetings in the past he and his family faced ruin.

It was, he emphasized, grossly unfair that he could be driven from public life and into ruin when he was totally innocent, and that he should become the victim of malevolent gossip, which was threatening to do to him what shortly before had been done to one of his colleagues. He meant the innocent Galbraith, whose persecution was at the same time being discussed at the Radcliffe tribunal.

Profumo went further. He insisted vehemently that he had not committed adultery and would sue no matter who had made the assertion. If he could identify a gossip-monger, he would sue. If anything was published he would sue.

It must have been impossible for the two law officers not to believe their colleague. Their reasoning must have been that anyone who was prepared to go to the High Court to take action and go into the witness box, for that is what it would entail, and state categorically on oath that he had not committed adultery with this slip of a girl who was known to sleep around, must be telling the truth. No-one in their right mind would do such a thing if they were in the wrong. The penalty for anyone found to be lying and perverting the course of justice was even worse than ruin in public life. It meant a long time in prison.

1 February: Macmillan was away in Rome trying to get Britain into the Common Market despite France's General de Gaulle turning down the application. So when Mark Chapman-Walker, former director of research at Tory Central Office and now a senior executive with the *News of the World*, rang his old friend John Wyndham, the Prime Minister's principal private secretary, to say he had some information vital for the government, it was Wyndham who listened to what he had to say and another of the secretarial staff who took a note. It read:

> The object of the call concerned a security matter ... Mr Profumo had compromised himself with a girl who was involved with a negro in a case about attempted murder ... this girl's story has been sold to the Daily Mirror Group and it will include passages in which she was involved with Mr Profumo and in which the Russian naval attaché also figured ... Profumo is alleged to have met the girl Kolania through Lord Astor at Cliveden where they chased her naked around the swimming pool ... it is also alleged that (1) Kolania got into this company through the agency of a Mr Ward who is a psychopathic specialist of Wimpole Street; (2) Mr Profumo, visiting Kolania in Mr Ward's house, passed in the passage the Russian naval attaché on his way from Kolania; (3) Kolania has two letters on War Office paper signed 'J' although it is not suggested that these letters are anything more than ones of assignation.

It was a fair and accurate summary of what had happened (and a bombshell) except it did not say that the naked romps around Cliveden, the fornicating in Ward's flat, the passing in the passage and the letters had happened eighteen months earlier and that Ivanov had left the country. Kolania was Keeler and 'a Mr Ward' (it was curious how everyone used this description when referring to Ward; Macmillan was to use it later as a form of contemptuous abuse) was Dr Stephen Ward.

Wyndham immediately called in the deputy Director-General of the security service to tell him and to ask him what he knew. He told Wyndham who was who, how Profumo had tried to get a 'D' notice slapped on the matter, and other details. The two men agreed that the first step was to see Profumo and ask him whether there was any truth in it and whether he should tender his resignation. Wyndham also said he would tell the Chief Whip and the Prime Minister when he returned from Italy.

Wyndham saw Profumo later that evening and again Profumo denied it. He said that he had been in continuous touch with the law officers and suggested that Wyndham should not bother the Prime Minister at that stage. Wyndham said he should see the Chief Whip without delay and Profumo agreed to this. He also said that his solicitor was seeing Keeler at her request since she said she was in trouble.

2/3 February: The weekend was spent in trying to find a way to stop Keeler's story being published after the trial, which was to take place on Tuesday and loomed like a giant cloud over Ward, Astor and Profumo. Ward's counsel and Profumo's solicitor had the idea that a writ for slander (because Keeler had told several people her story by now) might stop publication. It needed a good deal of work to prepare such an action. Their first thought was that Keeler should have a solicitor of her own: she had been given the number of one by Profumo's legal advisers, but they had the impression she was after money. In the end she chose her own and on the Sunday afternoon, the day before Keeler went to see him, he was briefed by Rees-Davies.

By the end of the weekend the negotiations were clearly heading towards two objectives: that Keeler should withdraw from her newspaper contract so that her story could not possibly be published (and it had to be passed by the paper's lawyer first), and that she should go away immediately after the Edgecombe trial. In return she was to be paid money for the loss of her contract and her expenses.

There was one final piece of action on Sunday. In the evening Profumo took his solicitor to the Attorney-General's home. The solicitor made it plain that Profumo had told him the same story as he had told the two law officers – that his relationship with the girl was totally innocent.

Thirty years on, it is still impossible to say why Profumo persisted with his story, which was a lie. He will not say. He has kept silent all these years, refusing each request for an interview or article with politeness so one can only assume or guess. I have always felt that he thought he would get away with it. It was all so far in the past, the girl had gone downhill so that her word against his was no great threat, her account had changed from time to time while his was a steadfast denial. At this stage in the story he had lied to old friends and colleagues and his solicitor, with the Chief Whip and the Prime Minister still to face. He could have gone back because it was by no means public knowledge despite Lewis's efforts, but Profumo chose not to.

4 February: Late in the afternoon Keeler went to see her solicitor. They talked and he then rang Profumo's solicitor, to set out the ground for the negotiations. Keeler's man said she did not want to harm the minister but she had no-one to turn to for financial assistance except the newspaper, who had offered payment for her story. If she did not continue with the story, she had nothing. The trial was due the next day and she intended going away after that. She was to get between £1,000 and £1,500 for her story.

Then they got down to serious business. Keeler wanted £3,000 and Profumo's solicitor said he would take instructions. A few minutes later, Keeler's man rang to say that she wanted more, another £2,000, so she could get a house for her parents. Keeler later explained to Lord Denning (who carried out an inquiry at Macmillan's request in the summer) that this was not blackmail. If she was into that – and she insisted rightly that she was not – she could have asked for £50,000. When £3,000 was mentioned she said no because she wanted to move her parents, so she raised the price.

Profumo's side never rang Keeler's solicitor. Instead Profumo, advised by his solicitor who had taken the advice of Queen's Counsel, went to see the Attorney-General again. He told Hobson about Keeler's request for the money. Hobson

regarded it as a serious matter and said the facts should be put
before the Director of Public Prosecutions. Hobson was now
convinced that Profumo was telling him the truth. Any man who
was prepared not only to sue for libel but to prosecute over
£5,000, could not be lying. Hobson knew what had occurred
when Profumo had seen Redmayne earlier in the day.

Wyndham was there too for the midday meeting. Profumo
went through the story again, insisting that everyone was
wearing bathing suits at Cliveden, that he went round to Ward's
flat to have a 'giggle' while enjoying a drink with the young
people who met there (not the kind to take a constituency
meeting but the kind of theatrical group he was used to mixing
with), that he had written Keeler one note and had given her a
cigarette lighter because she admired it. The gift alone should
have been enough to create a major doubt about his story, but it
passed without comment.

Now, said Profumo, the girl wanted money and refused to say
that any of the stories she had given to the papers were untrue.
His lawyers had advised him to do nothing but wait and see if
the paper published, and if it was libellous, sue them – which he
would do. The law officers had advised him in the same way and
he had made a full report to the head of the security service.
Should he now tell the Prime Minister?

The Chief Whip did not think that was necessary nor that he
should resign over the current rumours, but he would have to if
they were true. The thing to do was to wait and see what was
published, and then act if necessary.

Profumo then told more. He said that he had never met
Ivanov at Ward's flat and had seen him only at Cliveden and at
the Yuri Gagarin reception. He remembered that because
Ivanov had promised to get him and Valerie a vodka, but had
gone off never to be seen again.

Redmayne digested all this and then asked the obvious
question: 'Well, look, you know nobody would believe that you
did not sleep with her?

Profumo answered with hestitation: 'Yes, I know they
wouldn't believe it, but it happens to be true that I didn't sleep
with her.' He kept on insisting that this was the case, and that he
was just waiting for the chance to sue.

It is easy now to say that the Chief Whip should have said
something like, 'Come off it, don't be so bloody stupid, are you

really trying to tell me that all you did when you were with this girl was to talk?' Profumo could have admitted all and resigned and let it blow over. But he did not. Like the law officers, Redmayne accepted the word of a man who was prepared to repeat his story in the witness box in the High Court.

Profumo must have thought he had got away with it completely when Macmillan returned from Italy and was briefed on what had gone on between Profumo and the various senior officials of the government, and the allegations about the girl and his denial. Macmillan accepted the denial absolutely. Later he gave two reasons why he had done so: he felt that it was better to let Profumo see colleagues in the same age group and if there was anything in the rumours, he would tell them rather than an older man like Macmillan. The other reason made sense too, that if he was to question a minister there was no going back. The Prime Minister either believed him or not. If he did not, that was the end of the minister's career.

5 February: The day that the trio so dreaded began with good news. The Edgecombe trial was adjourned because the minicab driver, who was an important witness, had a heart attack (from which he died) and so there was a breathing space.

That did not deter Profumo. He went to see the Director of Public Prosecutions, whose view, after hearing all the facts about the request for money, was that he should not prosecute because it would be difficult to prove Keeler's intent in asking for money.

It was, looking back, a breathtaking move by Profumo. This was not just a threat to an ex-lover, only twenty years old; this involved one of the major legal figures in the land who had the weight and the majesty of the law behind him. Profumo was prepared to lie to save his skin wherever he went, to whomsoever he spoke.

At the same time, Keeler's solicitor saw Ward's counsel and mentioned that she wanted 'five'. Ward's man thought that would be all right, thinking it meant five hundred, not five thousand. Ward agreed and borrowed it from Lord Astor, telling him it was for legal expenses, but when it became clear to Keeler that it was only £500 she was going to get, she turned him down flat. She was never to get a penny of it.

Five hundred was the figure that Ward had in his mind. He

was not trying to cheat her, he just could not work out such a complicated deal. He got the cheque from Astor, who said he could repay it sometime or work it off with treatment for sprains, bruises or hunting accidents. As Keeler, from whom he was now estranged did not want it, Ward paid off his rent and other debts.

Keeler was extremely angry, and with considerable justification. She signed the proofs of her story three days later.

Having sorted out the money, Ward went round to Marylebone police station after telling them on the phone that two photographs had been stolen from his flat. They were shots at the swimming pool at Cliveden, one taken by Profumo showing Ward with three girls, one of whom was Keeler, and on the back the minister had written 'The new Cliveden set, J': the other was taken by someone else and showed Profumo with two girls, one of whom was Keeler. Neither picture has ever been seen again and the thief was never caught. Ward was asked to go to the police station to make a short statement. The policeman who took the statement passed his notes on to his superior. They read:

· Dr Ward said that, if this matter, including the association between Mr Profumo and Miss Keeler became public, it might very well 'bring down' the Government. He also added that he had no personal liking to see it go out of office in this way. He also said that he was aware that Miss Keeler had sold her life story to the Sunday Pictorial newspaper and that a number of names would be mentioned. Ward also said that he was a close friend of the naval attaché of the Soviet Embassy, who frequently visited him and who was known in diplomatic circles as 'Foxface'. He produced a photograph which he said had been taken at an official Iron Curtain party and in it he appeared standing alongside 'Foxface'. He also said he had mentioned the matter to a member of MI5.

The police at Marylebone put together the Keeler and Ward statements which were sent to Special Branch who considered the matter. They regarded themselves as guardians of security and not minister's morals. They considered that as the security services knew the gist of the matter, and as Ivanov had gone, there was no need to take any further action. This was much the view of the security services, so there it was left.

Everything, if only they had known it, was not yet lost for Profumo and Ward; even at this stage, if only they had had the power or sense to see, they could have averted the tragedies that were to follow.

Lewis by this time was watching with amazement and, no doubt, amusement, the way his planting of information was going. He was playing his game as a loner. He was now moving on a different level. He was not going to let anyone except Wigg and Townsend know what he was up to. He had friends who were mixing with Ward and they were reporting back. But even they did not know the extent of Lewis's involvement. Keeler had cursed him and Ward was to curse him to the grave later, but others just did not know.

So, by *5 February* following ten days of hectic activity, these events had taken place:

1   Attempts by Profumo and Ward to have Keeler silenced, either by threat or offer of money, had come to nothing.

2   The press was now in open warfare with the government. Two journalists, Reg Foster of the *Daily Sketch* and Brendan Mulholland of the *Daily Mail* had been gaoled for three and six months respectively, for contempt of court. They refused to reveal their sources in the Vassall affair (over which the Prime Minister had reluctantly accepted the resignation of the completely innocent Thomas Galbraith) and although lawyers argued that the long-standing freedom of the press was at stake if they were forced to reveal their sources and that a constitutional right was at risk, the High Court ruled that withholding information needed in the administration of justice was not a privilege allowed to anyone including the press. The war between the government and the Fourth Estate, the press, was now out in the open and what was to follow depended much on that. There was no mercy for a government on the run and none was shown even by its traditional supporters.

3   The police, the Special Branch director, and the Director-General of MI5 and some in MI6 knew about Profumo, the girl and the Russian, partly because of a statement taken about the Edgecombe shooting and mainly because Lewis had told them, either in person or anonymously.

4   Profumo had lied consistently to his senior colleagues and his solicitor. It was Profumo's lies that kept the matter going.

Looking back now, it is clear that if Profumo had told the truth in face of the evidence that his colleagues had; if they had not been prepared to accept his word and his protestations; if the trial of Edgecombe had gone ahead with the £5,000 that Keeler had asked for in her pocket; if the *Sunday Pictorial* had just dumped the story because she would not sign – then it would have been the word of a girl who was into the drugs and West Indian scene against the straight denial of a minister. There were no witnesses, just a letter that might or might not mean anything.

The Home Secretary was not told because no-one thought it was any of his business and nor was the Prime Minister who was the head of the security services, told of the Russian link, only of Profumo's denial about the girl.

So on and on the snowball rolled, and Lewis was delighted.

14

THE SNOWBALL ROLLS ON

Incredibly, all was still not lost. There was the whole of February and a few days in March before the trial for Profumo to step forward and say that it was a lie, that he had slept with Keeler, that he was sorry and would resign.

Ward had stopped the papers. He had persuaded both the *Sunday Pictorial* and the *News of the World* that Keeler was untrustworthy and that they should not take her word. Instead, he suggested, he could provide them with an article showing the dangers facing young girls like Keeler, straight from her home, two railway carriages in Wraysbury, Berkshire, who came to London and got involved in sex. He did not offer the information that such girls were his bread and butter, and that they might end up in bed with the likes of millionaire property magnate Charles Clore, racketeer landlord and slum harassment supremo Peter Rachman, and insurance swindler Dr Emil Savundra as Keeler and Rice-Davies did.

The papers, unaware of Ward's secret life of depravity, accepted the stories for use after the Edgecombe trial in March. The *Sunday Pictorial* was not bothered. The journalists knew they could never get Keeler's story past the lawyers. It was still the word of a model girl in trouble with West Indian men and with a taste for reefers and low life against a minister of the Crown. They dropped the story, probably with relief, and returned the original of the 'Darling' letter to Profumo's solicitor, keeping a copy in the safe which they were to use later when it was possible.

For the rest of the month and well into March the papers were chasing hard to try to get into the story. Everyone had heard the rumours by now, thanks to Lewis. He was providing a steady drip of information amongst the circles in which he mixed, still obtaining news from his friends who saw Ward, from his contacts in the police, but not from Wigg, because it was Lewis who was supplying him. The press were able to find out more because they had men on the ground everywhere. Keeler and Rice-Davies had told small parts of the story, Ward other bits, side players added extra bits, cafe and pub society contributed more, so that the picture became more in focus. However much the press knew, it fell far short of what they could have found out if only Profumo and Ivanov had opened their mouths. The shadow of Lewis and libel damages hung over the press all the time.

Wigg had no such difficulty. Lewis provided him with a dossier of everything he knew, and that was plenty. Denning was to say of him, following his meeting with Keeler on 23 December: 'John Lewis was at once alive to the importance of the matter from a security point of view. He told Mr George Wigg MP about it. And from that time onwards he kept Mr Wigg fully informed of every development. They had conversations almost daily. John Lewis was so interested that he, in March 1963, got his own agent to investigate in the person of a journalist who spent much of his time in Stephen Ward's flat.'

There was nothing wrong in that. Journalists were swapping information between themselves and with those involved. Lewis was not one of the principals and, as we know, reporters were very wary of him. When Denning made his comments about Lewis in the report, published in September, he was well aware of the link between Lewis and Ward in the past. He stated: 'In the course of conversation the shooting was discussed. Stephen Ward's name was mentioned and at once old memories revived. John Lewis and Stephen Ward had been engaged actively in litigation in 1954 and 1955 and there was no love lost between them.'

Denning had been told this by Lewis himself when he gave evidence in July or August. By that time Lewis had done all the damage he could but even then Denning did not make the connection between Lewis's hatred for Ward and everything that followed.

Wigg had no inkling when Lewis brought him his dossier, compiled with loving hatred, that his aim was to fix Ward once and for all. It was a comprehensive report, containing gossip, flimsy fact and rumours of wild sex orgies. There were stories of coupling, tripling and four in a bed; of two-way mirrors (one in Ward's new flat which was put up by Hamilton to watch his guests, was broken by Rice-Davies when she hurled a shoe at Rachman during a row); of whipping and other forms of flagellation at parties; and of groups of well-known people meeting for the joys of fornication and other naked and clothed romps. It also had detailed information about Ward, Profumo, Ivanov and Keeler, and the possibility of a security risk, which, Lewis stressed, was his prime mover.

Wigg, usually so decisive and forthright, dithered. It was not because of any fear of taking action. It was because he was a decent man and he did not want to hurt Profumo. He was not going to attack on moral grounds, that was certain in his mind. In ordinary circumstances he would have gone to the man and told him what he knew. But Profumo was different. Wigg considered he had let him down, he was untrustworthy. It was to cost Profumo his public life. Wigg studied the dossier and prepared his own from it.

There was little more that Lewis could do at that time except watch and wait. He wanted to see which way Wigg would play it, whether Commander Townsend would do anything about his information, what the inland revenue would do, what the security services would do, although he knew via Ward that they had been around. He guessed the inland revenue would already be looking at his bank account and his tax return. They always did.

All through February nothing happened after the fevered activity at the start of the month. Profumo kept silent. He had every opportunity to avoid the disaster but he did nothing to avert it.

I believe that he thought he was safe, that his word would be accepted against Keeler, particularly now that Ivanov was out of the country. Ward was not going to say anything nor were any of his friends in the crowd he and his wife mixed with. There still was no proof.

Wigg went on dithering until Sunday 10 March. He was up in his constituency and he had heard wrongly as it turned out, that two Sunday papers had stories about the affair and were going to publish them. He had good grounds for thinking this. On 8 March the current weekly issue of *Westminster Confidential*, a political news-letter with a small circulation amongst those who worked in the Palace of Westminster was published. It was the work of Andrew Roth, an expert journalist who was very well informed. He had not only picked up the Profumo Affair, but was prepared to use it. He wrote:

> That Was The Government That Was!' [from the current TV hit show of the time.]
> 'That is certain to bring down the government!' a Conservative MP wailed, 'and what will my wife say?' This combination of tragedy and tragi-comedy came from the efforts of this MP to check with newspapermen on the story which had run like wildfire through Parliament.

Roth then recounted the details of the rumour of how the shooting had happened, and how the girls were trying to sell their stories to the Sunday papers. Then he reached the nitty-gritty. He said:

> One of the choicest bits in the stories was a letter, apparently signed Jack, on the stationery of the Secretary for W-r. The allegation by this girl was not only that this minister who has a famous actress as a wife, was her client but also the Soviet military attaché, apparently a Colonel Ivanov. The famous actress wife, of course, would sue for divorce, the scandal ran.
> Who was using the girl to 'milk' whom of information – the W-r Secretary or the Soviet military attaché – ran the minds of those primarily interested in security.
> It was probably knowledge about this story as well as the scandal concerning X (another Tory MP) and his young car-borrowing friend which led the Chief Whip, Brigadier Redmayne, to tell a correspondent with resignation: 'We have all the luck.'

It was the first occasion on which Profumo could sue. For some reason, neither he nor the Chief Whip nor the Attorney-General heard about it for five days and when they did they discussed legal action but thought the circulation of the news sheet was too small; they should wait for a paper with a bigger circulation to print the lie.

So on the Sunday Wigg, still undecided, went to a party at Barbara Castle's home (she was a minister in Wilson's government the next year and more to follow). He discussed it with her and Richard Crossman (later also to be a minister in the Wilson government and then to publish his diaries) who both said that it would do Labour no good and that he should leave it alone. They wanted nothing to rebound on them on the moral side; Wigg insisted it was a security issue.

Then Wigg got Wilson on his own. He was new at his job as leader. He was an extremely clever and adroit politician. Wigg told Wilson the story, the link betwen Profumo and Ivanov, how the foreign press were going to blow the story wide open while the British press wavered on the beach, afraid to dive in. He explained the involvement with Ward and Keeler, the forthcoming trial of Edgecombe and the issues it raised. He said that the time had come for Wilson to press the government to make a statement and then to have a select committee in which the Prime Minister's responsibility for security should be included.

Wilson did not agree. In Wigg's words, he wanted to play it cool. He told Wigg that he should pursue the matter 'on his own responsibility' and Wigg went away to consider what to do next, having left Wilson a copy of his dossier.

First Wigg went to see an old friend to ask for his advice. The friend said that he should use his parliamentary privilege when the chance arose. That was what he had been given the privilege for, he said, echoing the words of Hugh Gaitskell over Vassall when Wigg too had asked for his advice.

On 8 March, Keeler went away on holiday to Spain with some friends. It was not known until the day of the trial that she had gone and was not going to turn up as the key witness on 14 March.

When Edgecombe stood in the dock and pleaded not guilty to shooting at Christine Keeler with intent to murder her, shooting at her with intent to cause grievous bodily harm, possessing a pistol with intent to endanger life and possessing an offensive weapon in a public place, the public had no idea that the failure of the main witness to appear – a failure which had nothing to do with the thirty-year-old salesman from Antigua, it was stressed – mattered anywhere else.

The jury heard that Keeler had lived with Edgecombe for a while and had then left. He tried to see her at Rice-Davies' flat but when she would not come out he fired five shots into the door and two at her when she appeared at the window.

Edgecombe said that he fired to try to get in after she

'contemptuously' threw a note at him. He never had any intention of shooting her.

The jury believed him and found him guilty only of possessing a pistol with intent to endanger life. They cleared him of wounding Lucky Gordon by slashing him with a razor. Edgecombe said he was not the man who did it.

He was sentenced to seven years by Mr Justice Thesiger, a judge noted for his severe sentences. He said:

> I think you were quite rightly convicted of possessing a firearm with intent to endanger life. You kept the pistol, you cleaned it and you set out on 14 December with it. You then tried to shoot your way into someone's flat and finally shot at the wall in the direction of the window.
>
> I think that if you had got that girl out you would have had a shot at her.
>
> There are too many cases of pistols together with quite a quantity of ammunition being in possession of unreliable people.
>
> That is what leads to cases of capital murder.

The *Daily Sketch* ran a big picture story of Rice-Davies and her life with Keeler and Ward.

Three days later the papers linked Keeler and Ivanov. A day later *The Times* ran a strong leader headed 'It is Happening Here' hitting back at those who were hostile to the press following Vassall and making the point that the executive, meaning the Cabinet, had taken over power from parliament. It said firmly that if journalists had to reveal their sources, they would dry up.

On 20 March Keeler's disappearance was mentioned before Mr Justice Lyell at the Old Bailey. No order was made for her to appear to explain why she had not turned up to give evidence, nor was it stated whether she would have to forfeit her £40 recognisance as a witness.

The next night, Thursday 21 March 1963, it all came out in the open in the House of Commons.

The House of Commons was debating the case of the two imprisoned journalists and just before 11 p.m. Wigg stood to speak. He had made up his mind. He had been pushed into this because another Labour MP, Ben Parkin, had made a double-talk remark at a committee, where he said 'There is the case of the missing model. We understand that a model can quite easily be obtained for the convenience of a minister of the Crown,' which baffled most people there as they were talking about London sewage. Later, journalists heard that Barbara Castle was to talk about a 'missing witness'.

Wigg said: 'The press can exercise freedom over its criticism of the executive, the opposition and Hon. Members – but it should have regard for the public good.

'I hold the view that neither the House of Commons nor the press could function satisfactorily unless there was present in both a respect for factual integrity.'

He referred to the Vassall tribunal, and stated that they had a job to do. He said:

They were not there in order to bring the mailed fist of totalitarianism into it but to do a job that the House of Commons had by unanimous resolution authorized them to do. If Hon. Members now grumble about the result, I ask them where they were on 14 November when we were raising our voices against this particular form of tribunal.

So far, so good. Here was a set of rumours that gained and gained in strength, consumed men's reputations – might, in fact, have destroyed them – and which here infringed on the security of the State.

But we are quite sure that the same thing is not happening again? There is not an Hon. Member in the House, nor a journalist in the press gallery, nor do I believe there is a person in the public gallery who, in the last few days, has not heard rumour upon rumour involving a member of the government front bench.

The press has got as near as it could – has shown itself willing to wound but afraid to strike. This all comes about because of the Vassall tribunal. In actual fact, these great press lords, these men who control great instruments of public opinion and of power, do not have the guts to discharge the duty that they are now claiming for themselves.

That being the case, I rightly use the privilege of the House of Commons – that is what it is given me for – to ask the Home Secretary who is the senior member of the government on the treasury bench now, to go to the dispatch box – he knows that the rumour to which I refer relates to Miss Christine Keeler and Miss Davies and a shooting by a West Indian – and, on behalf of the government, categorically deny the truth of these rumours.

On the other hand, if there is anything in them, I urge him to ask the Prime Minister to do what was not done in the Vassall case – set up a select committee so that these things can be dissipated, and the honour of the minister concerned freed from the imputation and innuendos that are being spread at the present time.

It is not good for a democratic state that rumours of this kind should spread and be inflated, and go on. Everyone knows what I am referring to, but up to now nobody has brought the matter into the open. I believe that the Vassall tribunal need never have been set up had the nettle been firmly grasped much earlier on. We have lost some time and I plead with the Home Secretary to use the dispatch box to clear up all the mystery and speculation over this particular case.

Some of the rumours by this time had it that Profumo or Astor or someone on Profumo's behalf, an allegation Profumo denied truthfully to the Attorney-General, was involved in Keeler's disappearance. All that had happened was that the *Sunday Pictorial* had told her that they were not going ahead with her story, and she was broke. She had also had enough. It is sometimes forgotten that she was still very young, not yet twenty-one, inexperienced in the ways of the world among much older and street-wise people, when all this fell around her. She had had a rough few months, going downhill by her own choice but still under Ward's influence. She had had a man after her with a gun, had been abandoned by her mentor and was now caught, thanks to Lewis, in a situation between a minister, a Russian spy, the press, a potential goldmine and all the pressures that meant. She just wanted to go away; and, with an attitude of to-hell-with-the-consequences, she went.

Wigg sat down and was followed by Dick Crossman, a war-time propaganda specialist and a leading light in the Labour party. He was an intellectual in the Gaitskell tradition. He said that the issue was not that the men in this case were journalists, but were citizens who had been hauled before a tribunal and being outrageously treated by it. He said: 'We are moving into another situation of a similar kind. Even by this evening the Paris newspapers will have published in full the rumours which are going round the House and the country and which are touched on from day to day by the press. It would have been wiser if we had established a select committee ten days ago. If we have tribunal procedure again we shall not achieve what we need.'

Both men had clearly made the point that the press were in the know but afraid to put what they knew in print. Wigg could have added that there was a good reason for that – the vicious libel laws that made publication such a terrible financial risk. It is all very well advising publish and be damned (Macmillan was to do it with Denning) if you have not got to pay the damages.

Then Barbara Castle, an outspoken, lifelong socialist, put forward her view, which really moved matters on for she gave more facts. She said:

> One of the grounds why the Home Secretary should exercise his discretion is that there is also a widespread belief that these two men are being punished for the failings of the press as a whole. Who was to decide when adventurous sensationalism was to the public good?
>
> Mr Wigg has referred to a current piece of adventurous sensationalism in which the press is currently involved. It would suit the book of many people to deplore the avidity with which the press was pursuing the question of where was Miss Christine Keeler, the vanished witness.

Barbara Castle, whose knowledge came from Wigg, who had been told by Lewis, went further: 'But what if there was something else of greater importance?' More: 'What if a perversion of justice was at stake?' Profumo must have been really worried by that.

She went on:

> The Clerk of the Criminal Court, Mr Leslie Boyd, was reported in *The Times* as saying that if any member of the public knew where Miss Keeler was it was his or her duty to inform the police.
>
> If accusations were made that there were people in high places who did know and were not informing the police, was it not a matter of public interest that it should be brought to light?

The Home Secretary, Henry Brooke, whose tenure of office was marred by a run of unfortunate decisions over asylum and other matters, then had a swipe at Wigg and Castle before saying that although it gave him no pleasure that the two journalists were in gaol, he could find no grounds for using his prerogative to reduce the sentences. He said of the two Labour MPs: 'I do not propose to comment on rumours that have been raised under the cloak of privilege and safe from any action of law. Mr Wigg and Mrs Castle should seek other means of making these insinuations if they are prepared to substantiate them.'

Brooke made a bad mistake there. Wigg had said nothing that he could not repeat outside the House and nor had Barbara Castle. He made it clear that he was interested in the security side only. He had used the privilege he was given as an MP but he had made a statement that he could repeat outside without any trouble. Brooke had inflicted another wound on an angry member of the opposition who always went to a great deal of trouble to make sure he was fully in possession of the facts. The trouble was, as we shall shortly see, that Brooke in spite of being in charge of the Metropolitan police, knew nothing, absolutely nothing, about Profumo and what was going on.

Ward, whose story, 'The Model, MI5, the Russian Diplomat and Me', had appeared the previous Sunday, was sound asleep in bed when this happened. Lewis was at home and Profumo had gone home to bed, taking a dose of sleeping tablets to make him sleep well. He needed them, I imagine, because although he had told the Attorney-General a few days earlier that he had had nothing to do with the disappearance of Keeler, the rumours started again as soon as it was announced at the trial that she had vanished. He had also been seen by the Chief Whip shortly after Wigg had made his speech. Profumo had dropped in to see what was going on in the House on his way home from a dinner party.

His heart must have missed a beat when Redmayne accosted him and told him what had been said. He said: 'I must ask you point blank, did you or didn't you?' to which Profumo truthfully replied that he did not, because he had absolutely nothing to do with Keeler's disappearance.

It was 12.40 a.m. on 22 March when Profumo and his wife went to bed. Redmayne had told him he might have to make a statement but had told him to go home. But once he had gone, the Chief Whip had second thoughts and decided that the best way to deal with this was for the minister to make a personal statement in the House. He woke Macmillan from sleep, who also agreed that this was the best course.

A personal statement is rarely made by an MP, but when it is, it is accepted without question that what the member says is true, absolutely, completely, without any exception of fact, honestly true. No-one had ever been known to lie on such an occasion. No statement from a witness box, dock, under oath in a statement or affidavit, sworn on any religious book, compares fully with the words that a member utters to his colleagues in the House. In 1963 there was no argument. If a member stood up and said something, it was true and correct. There was absolutely no doubt in anyone's mind.

So, after the debate, at half past one in the morning, the Chief Whip asked the Leader of the House, the late Iain Macleod, later Chancellor of the Exchequer, master bridge player and loyal friend to the Profumos before his early and tragic death, to come to his room. Then, over a drink, the Attorney-General, who had also arrived, stressed strongly that Profumo should deny the rumours and sue if anyone printed them. But when should he make his denial? They all agreed that it would have to be done on the Friday morning sitting of the House (it later caused a gasp of astonishment from the deputy prime minister, Rab Butler, that such a momentous statement should be made when most MPs were on their way to their constituencies for the weekend) to thwart any attempt by the Sunday papers to do any muck-raking. So they called back William (now Lord) Deedes, the Minister without Portfolio, in charge of information and later editor of the *Daily Telegraph*, from his home because he too, like the other three, had been in the Chamber during the debate. Then the Solicitor-General came in. The only other senior government officer who had been in the House during the debate and who was not there was the Home Secretary, because no-one at this impromptu meeting thought to ask him. He had never been involved in any of the earlier discussions with Profumo, and all the others believed wrongly that it was not really a security matter.

They then decided to have Profumo back to draft the statement. It was agreed that his solicitor should be there because if Profumo was later to sue (as he did), then it would have to be in a form which would not prejudice litigation. It did occur to the Attorney-General that Profumo might have said something to his solicitor, under the cloak of professional privilege, that he might not have said to his colleagues. They need not have worried. Profumo had lied to his solicitor as well.

A messenger was sent round to Profumo's house, because there was no answer to a telephone call. They were both drugged with sleeping pills. The banging on the door finally woke them at a quarter to three and Profumo dressed and went back to the House. His wife Valerie later told Denning: 'We were so groggy. All the man said, who came was 'Look, you have got to come back to the House,' and I remember Jack groping his way round and saying 'I must have a clean shirt,' and trying to push the cuff-links through.'

Both Valerie and her husband believe that this early morning summons did lead to Profumo going ahead with the personal statement. She told Denning:

> This is terribly important. I would like to make a statement about this. I just simply know that, if it had not been for the concatenation of circumstances of timing that day, and that early morning, Jack would never have made that statement. I was there and I know about the sleeping pills and the tiredness and the fact that we were really groping round the house, letting in strange people and getting through loads of reporters still on the doorstep. I sat up in the drawing room with the cat on my lap until he came back at 4.45 a.m. and he said; 'This is the statement' ... I am sure that had we had time, as husband and wife, instead of ... what a time gun.

She presumably meant the pressure to make the statement at once instead of leaving them time to discuss it. Profumo himself hinted that if he had been more awake things might have been different. But he went to join his colleagues and found that his solicitor had arrived before him.

The five ministers wanted to quash the three rumours in one go. Only one – the disappearance of Keeler and the suggestion that he had something to do with it – had been raised in the chamber, but there were the other two, the accusation of adultery and the possible security issue if he had been sharing her with the Russian. The other five Tories all accepted his word that there was no truth in any of them. Perhaps if they had not been so ready to accept his word and had thought more about the association with a girl of easy favours (even if she had been different when he met her), they might have realized that any average man would automatically think that the minister had

had the girl. But they did not think that way. They wanted him to stop the rumours, and a personal statement was the way to do it.

In hindsight, they should have stopped and thought: let's wait until the morning and in that time we'll make a few inquiries, such as asking the Metropolitan Police whether they know anything about Keeler and Profumo, and perhaps asking the *Sunday Pictorial* if we could have a look at the letter they have. Maybe, if Keeler has told them a story, we could see what that says, strictly off the record, just for guidance.

We know now that if they had done so, they would have seen Keeler's statement to Detective Sergeant Burrows on 26 January, nearly two months earlier; what Ward said to the police on 5 February; and the story Keeler was selling to the *Sunday Pictorial* in which everything that Profumo was denying was shown to be true.

But they did not. The Attorney-General and the Chief Whip and Profumo were to say later that if they had had those in front of them, everyone's view would have been different. But Profumo persisted with his lie and his colleagues believed him. The statement was approved by Macmillan who knew the rumours from early February.

Shortly before eleven on Friday 22 March Profumo rose in the House. To show that they supported him he was flanked by the Prime Minister, the Leader of the House and the Attorney-General. Such solid support gave extra strength, if any was needed, to the statement.

Profumo, smartly dressed and groomed as ever, did not hesitate. He lied, only once, but he did the unforgivable. He said:

> With permission, Sir, I wish to make a personal statement.
>
> I understand that in the debate on the Consolidated Fund Bill last night, under protection of parliamentary privilege, the Hon. Gentlemen the Members for Dudley (Mr Wigg) and for Coventry, East (Mr Crossman), and the Hon. Lady the Member for Blackburn (Mrs Castle), opposite, spoke of rumours connecting a minister with a Miss Keeler and a recent trial at the Central Criminal Court. It was alleged that people in high places might have been responsible for concealing information concerning the disappearance of a witness and the perversion of justice.

I understand that my name has been connected with the rumours about the disappearance of Miss Keeler.

I would like to take this opportunity of making a personal statement about these matters.

I last saw Miss Keeler in December 1961, and I have not seen her since. I have no idea where she is now. Any suggestion that I was in any way connected with or responsible for her absence from the trial at the Old Bailey is wholly and completely untrue.

My wife and I first met Miss Keeler at a house party in July 1961, at Cliveden. Among a number of people there was Dr Stephen Ward, whom we already knew slightly, and a Mr Ivanov, who was an attaché at the Russian Embassy.

The only other occasion that my wife or I met Mr Ivanov was for a moment at the official reception for Major Gagarin at the Soviet Embassy.

My wife and I had a standing invitation to visit Dr Ward.

Between July and December 1961 I met Miss Keeler on about half a dozen occasions at Dr Ward's flat, when I called to see him and his friends. Miss Keeler and I were on friendly terms. There was no impropriety whatsoever in my acquaintanceship with Miss Keeler.

Mr Speaker, I have made this personal statement because of what was said in the House last evening by the three Hon. Members and which, of course, was protected by privilege. I shall not hesitate to issue writs for libel and slander if scandalous allegations are made or repeated outside the House.

He sat down. There was no going back now. It was in the open and he was stuck with it. There was only one lie – that there was 'no impropriety whatsoever' with Keeler. It was the least important fact and not vital but it was the one that finished him.

To show that as far as he was concerned that was an end of it, and the papers could print at their peril, he went to the races at Sandown Park in the afternoon with his wife and was photographed with the Queen Mother. The picture was in all the papers. Later the Profumos were snapped dancing at a top night spot, happy and loving.

But that, of course, was by no means the end of it. The snowball that Lewis had started in January was now enormous. Nothing was going to stop it or melt it now and Lewis was to see to that as well.

On the same day, Ward went on television to say he endorsed

Profumo's statement. On Saturday 23 March, Keeler was found in Spain. She was to say to the *Daily Express* (who paid her £2,000 for her story) then that there was nothing wrong in her friendship with Profumo. She said: 'What Profumo says is quite correct. I have not been in his company since 1961.' A few days later she told the *News of the World* that 'certainly both he and his wife were friends of mine. But it was a friendship no-one can criticize.' The *News of the World* paid her £100 for that, and were later to have two more giant bites of the cherry, when her story was quite different.

On the Monday, Wigg, who said after the statement that there was 'black rage in his heart', went on television to say that security was the main consideration. He was one of several who did not believe Profumo, for the simple reason that he had been pumped with information by Lewis for three months which told him that it was just not true. Ward also knew the statement was a lie and he had rung to fix an appointment with Wigg for the next day. The old warrior wondered what that would bring.

Lewis gave the knife one final twist. So far his information to the police, through his visit to Commander Townsend, and his anonymous call, had been more general than specific; he had suggested that Ward was living off the immoral earnings of girls and that he was being protected by people in high places who were using the girls. This time he excelled himself. He put in writing facts, details of meetings, names and addresses, and compiled a dossier of what had been going on. It was complete enough to be taken seriously, and it was sent up to the Commissioner, Sir Joseph Simpson. It was on his desk, but unread, when he was summoned to a meeting which the Home Secretary had requested so that the Commissioner and Dick White, the head of security, could put him in the picture about Stephen Ward. Brooke believed Profumo, was suspicious about Ward and had absolutely no idea what had been going on.

The next day, Lewis went down to the House of Lords to hear the judgment on his appeal. The Lords were much of the same mind as the Court of Appeal. They felt that the size of the damages awarded, which they considered ridiculously out of proportion to the injury suffered by Lewis and his company, was excessive. They said that for them ever to be justified there would have to be evidence of a very different kind from that given in the two cases. They also felt that the innuendo that

Lewis and his company had read into the article should not have been put to the jury to consider, without the judge saying whether it was actually capable of bearing each of the defamatory meanings Lewis had put forward. The Lords ordered a new trial on the grounds of misdirection by the judge to the jury on the meaning of innuendo.

The ruling was business ruin for Lewis. His vast libel damages were disappearing like a ship over the horizon. He had a shrewd suspicion that he might well lose the retrial and even if he did win, his damages would be considerably reduced. If he did lose, the costs would be astronomical, and the loser paid all in this kind of action. He asked his lawyers to start talking with the two papers. There might be a solution that way.

While they did so, there was Ward to fry: and the cooking was going very well indeed.

15

AVALANCHE

On the morning of 26 March, Wigg discovered for the first time that there was a connection between Lewis and Ward. Anonymously, inevitably, someone, and it almost certainly was Lewis, sent Wigg an excerpt from the Lewis divorce case nine years earlier. The difference was, and Wigg was not to know this, that it had been doctored: it suggested that Ward was a witness and that the judge had described Ward as a far from attractive witness, 'one on whose word not the slightest reliance would be placed as regards any point on which he was called'. It was not Ward of whom the judge spoke so unfairly, but Freddy Mullally. Lewis had swapped names.

By the time Ward went to see Wigg that evening, the colonel had formed a poor view of him. The meeting, at which Ward arrived 'shaking like a jelly', did not improve the impression. Ward burbled on, talking about Ivanov and Cuba and his friendship with Ivanov and Profumo, and how they both knew Keeler, but there was nothing improper in that in any way. He told Wigg in a long and wide-ranging speech all about Edgecombe and Lucky Gordon, his relations with the press, and how Keeler and a friend of hers were now planning to sell stories to the papers.

Ward insisted that his practice as an osteopath was being ruined and that – and this seemed to be the thrust of the conversation – he was getting nothing out of protecting Profumo's reputation. Wigg detected a flaw in the story. Ward said he had last seen Ivanov before Christmas. If that were true, the Russian, knowing what was going on, would have left the country long before 29 January.

After hearing out Ward, Wigg decided that Profumo was not

a security risk: the security people knew all about the Ivanov – Profumo – Ward triangle and the police knew all about Edgecombe and Gordon. Wigg wrote it down in another dossier which he passed on to Harold Wilson, who had already plucked the Ward letter about Cuba – 'I was the intermediary' – from the file.

The next day the Home Secretary held his meeting with the police and security forces. It was White who told the Home Secretary the secret which had been kept from ministers throughout all the to-ing and fro-ing, all the Profumo questioning, all the MI5 and MI6 watching and trailing: Ward had asked Keeler to ask Profumo for information about the Americans intention to provide the West Germans with the bomb.

Using hindsight again, it is almost unbelievable that senior government officials, experts in espionage, did not mention that a minister of the Crown was sharing a young lady with a Russian spy, a great friend of a well-known left-wing sympathizer called Ward who was also suspected of providing girls to the gentry. The reason may be that when Hollis told Macmillan excitedly that they had got Vassall, instead of receiving praise, he had his arse kicked. Macmillan told him that if his gamekeeper shot a fox, he did not hang it up outside the master of foxhounds' drawing room but buried it out of sight. He said that it was not possible to shoot a spy as had been done in the war: you had to try him. It was better, thought the wily old Prime Minister, to discover the spy and then attempt to control him. It was a thought, delivered as a reprimand, that did the rounds in the top circles. So those in the know decided not to tell Macmillan what was going on about the security aspect: better to play down the Profumo Affair rather than incur his wrath again. In any case, it was all over by the time it came out into the open. Their attempts to turn Ivanov came to nothing, the minister had stopped bedding the girl over a year before. Ward had served his purpose as a potential spy and was about to get his come-uppance from the police.

To make matters even more silly, Brooke did not know that he was the first minister to be told. He just thought he was being kept up to date so he did not bother to tell any other minister. He assumed they all knew. How he reconciled this with Profumo's insistence that he had not slept with Keeler, it is impossible to guess. He must have been naive indeed, if he really believed that Profumo's friendship with Keeler was such that they merely chatted about such high-blown matters as the Cold War and when the Americans were going to give the Germans the bomb.

White said that if the allegations about the bomb were true, there might be grounds for prosecuting Ward under the Official Secrets Act. However, he thought the witnesses in such a prosecution – such as Keeler – might prove to be unreliable so they were not inclined to pursue the matter, a course with which Brooke agreed.

White also insisted that the security service's interest in the matter was limited to Ivanov and those he met and it was not their business to be involved with what Ward got up to with the girls. However, the Home Secretary then asked the Metropolitan Police Commissioner whether there was any police interest in Ward and Simpson said there would probably be grounds for prosecution if the police were able to get the full story. He doubted whether they would succeed in doing this.

Simpson went back to his office to consider this and was handed the anonymous 'Lewis' letter which he read with great interest. He was also handed the notes of the anonymous phone calls. The main letter was dated 25 March perfectly timed to drop in the middle of all the muddled thinking about Profumo.

The accusations went far beyond the titbits which Lewis had been providing on and off for years. They were substantial enough to require an investigation. The officers were under the control of Commander Arthur Townsend, the man to whom Lewis had told the story back in January. The two detectives who bore the brunt of the investigation were Detective Chief Inspector Samuel Herbert and his Detective Sergeant John Burrows. It involved questioning over 130 witnesses, mainly friends and girl-friends of Ward and others whom he had picked from the streets to perform services for friends in his flat. They discovered something his friends did not know, that he was leading a double life, mixing in high society with his nymphets and dredging the gutter for his own satisfaction. It was not a pretty picture which was later painted of such a gregarious and pleasant-seeming man.

The investigation began with first of twenty-six interviews with the prime witness, Christine Keeler, who was by now

completely baffled by what was going on. She had arrived back
from Spain to go to the Old Bailey flanked by *Daily Express*
outriders, to be fined her £40 recognisance that she had
forfeited by going to Spain and missing the Edgecombe trial. At
the same time, the security services had a look in their files. Lo
and behold, they found nothing to support a prosecution of
Ward, nothing that the Director of Public Prosecutions
considered was worth following and which would stand up in
court.

By the end of an extraordinary March, Michael Eddowes, the
solicitor who was the first to hear Keeler's story about her affair
with Profumo, sent a letter to the police saying that Keeler had
told him that it was Ivanov who had asked the girl to get
information from Profumo about the bomb, a line that was
always denied by Keeler.

Wilson had sent Macmillan Ward's letter from the Cuban
crisis during which the osteopath claimed he had acted as 'an
honest broker' between Russia and Britain. (To add an
espionage diversion, Edward Heath, the rising star of the
Tories, stood in the House as Lord Privy Seal to say that Philby
had legged it to Russia and that he was the Third Man).

April was a long month for Profumo. He must have known all
the time that the Labour party was gathering evidence. It was a
pity that the spirit of trust between two political rivals had been
broken and that Wigg did not trust his old sparring partner
enough to go to him and say that he (Wigg) had all the proof
necessary to show that Profumo was lying.

It was a long month for Ward, because he only slowly became
aware of what was happening; that an investigation had begun,
that girls were being questioned. He did not really appreciate
how serious it was until well into May. During April he tended
to dismiss the stories he heard from his circle. He was sure that
his big and powerful friends would protect him, people like Bill
Astor for whom he had done so much with his dexterous curing
fingers and the little poppets he had provided. Over the weeks
he realized that this was not going to happen. His clients fell
away, those who wanted to be sketched did not appear, and his
powerful friends dropped him like a hot potato. Astor came to
see him, but only to ask him to vacate the cottage because it was
not quite the scene, old boy, to have a tenant who was – how
should he put it? – not the sort of chap one wanted to be

associated with at the moment when the shit was flying and nasty questions were being asked about Russians and girls. He was sure Ward would understand and here were a few quid (£200) as recompense for all the work he had done on the cottage.

Astor was a heart-breaker but there were others. They closed ranks and went to ground in true Tory fashion. None of this nonsense about staying with the sinking ship. Just as they had disclaimed all knowledge in another famous case ten years earlier, people who enjoyed Astor's hospitality and Ward's girls would not admit to knowing where Cliveden was. Ten years before they had denied knowing the position of any public toilet in London when high-ranked people were involved in a (then) illegal homosexual scandal.

It was about this time, too, that Ward began to learn just what Lewis was doing to him. He had not linked Lewis with anything that was happening. He simply had no idea until those who knew Lewis and who also mixed with Ward mentioned that Lewis was sniffing around. Ward asked questions and discovered that his little baby had told Lewis all about Profumo and Ivanov, and that she had told the police. He also heard in a roundabout way, and it took time for him to hear all the story, that Lewis had gone to Wigg and told him too.

What Ward did not know was that Lewis had the ear of Commander Townsend, who was in overall charge of the inquiry to see whether there was any evidence against Ward which could be put before the Director of Public Prosecutions. It was often forgotten after the Ward trial, whatever view you took of his activities, that it was the Director who made the decision to prosecute, not the police. They were told to look and see if a crime was being committed and they found some evidence that this could be the case. But the decision on whether the evidence was strong enough was not theirs. It was the Director of Public Prosecutions who said that the case should go ahead.

So there was Ward waiting but, unlike Profumo, certain that nothing would be found against him. He was now starting to blame Lewis. This was the beginning of his totally justified complaints that Lewis was the architect of his downfall, the author of all his misfortunes.

In April, the snowball lay resting on a ledge for a while.

Wilson went to see the new President of the United States

and on his return sent Macmillan the Wigg/Lewis dossier with the links between Profumo and Ivanov and the world in which his Secretary of State for War had mixed. Macmillan took a week and wrote a languid and contemptuous letter back. It was a model of the careless manner in which Macmillan regarded the Affair in the early days, still believing his colleague implicitly: 'My Chief Whip has given to me the letter and enclosure from you dated 9 April dealing with George Wigg's conversation with a Mr Stephen Ward. I will ask the appropriate authorities to have an examination made of this information and will get in touch with you later on, if this seems necessary.'

It was a masterly stroke of rudeness. He was to be shown no mercy later. The reference to 'a Mr Stephen Ward' particularly irritated Wilson, who at that time was coming to the peak of his powers. He knew that Macmillan was fully aware of Dr Ward and his activities, both from Profumo and from information Wilson had supplied about Cuba. Wilson later said: 'It was symptomatic of the Prime Minister's indolent nonchalance.' It was also symptomatic of how far the Tories were unaware of what was going on and were quite unprepared for the public's revulsion when they discovered the lax morals of people in high places (which was to earn a severe rebuke from *The Times*), which in its turn was to lead to the downfall of the Tories in 1964. The net continued to tighten when Keeler made some of her statements to the police. In one she said: 'Stephen Ward had asked me to get information from Jack about the Americans giving the Germans the bomb. I did not get this information because it was ridiculous and could have been made in a joke.' It was not something the authorities thought at all funny. She also, and this was far worse from Profumo's point of view, gave a detailed description of the inside of his home and also his bedroom as supporting evidence that she had not just been in the house but had fornicated on the matrimonial bed.

At the same time Profumo was battling on, suing and gaining minor damages from the French picture magazine *Paris Match* for an ambiguous picture caption. The offending page was removed from copies sold in Britain. A few days later, he got a small sum from the Italian picture magazine *Tempo Illustrato* which had suggested that Profumo had had something to do with Keeler's disappearance from the Edgecombe trial which was quite untrue.

Also at the same time in Edinburgh, the bitter divorce action between the Duke and Duchess of Argyll ended with a 65,000 word judgment and victory for the Duke. One of four men cited appeared in a picture with the duchess, but the Polaroid snap had taken off his head and during the summer of rumour and tasty, sexy gossip many names were suggested. One senior government minister even went to the lengths of having a nude picture of himself taken to prove that it could not have been him.

On 18 April as Keeler, whose first autobiography had been published in the papers, left a flat in Devonshire Street in Marylebone, Gordon rushed her. A few minutes later the police hurried round to arrest him, but he had gone. He was arrested the next day, and on 3 May he was committed for trial at the Old Bailey, charged with causing Keeler grievous bodily harm. He insisted he had not hit Keeler and that there were two missing witnesses who would say just that. The police looked for them, but did not find them before his trial early in June.

By early summer Ward was beginning to realize how he was being trapped. He also saw quite clearly Lewis was behind it. He complained about it bitterly.

R. Barry O'Brien, the distinguished *Daily Telegraph* reporter who covered the story from start to finish and knew Ward very well, said:

> He always blamed Lewis. He said that he was the author of all his misfortunes. He said that Lewis was the starting point, bringing his whole world crashing down. He spoke at great length about Lewis and how it all stemmed from him, how unjustly he was accusing him.
>
> He regarded Lewis as an evil man who had pursued him unjustly with malevolence, but Ward did not seek vengeance because he was not that kind of man, but he was always going on about it.

He had good reason. Lewis was still hard at work. He was delighted with what he had done so far with the Labour party, but he was waiting for the real prizes to come later. He knew Profumo must crack (although he showed no sign of doing so, carrying on as enthusiastically and well with his job as ever) and be exposed, and from his inside information, he knew that Ward almost certainly would be tried.

On 7 May, Ward could stand it no more and decided he had to fight for his life. He phoned the Prime Minister's Private Secretary and that evening Timothy Bligh saw him with a senior member of the security forces there to listen.

Ward started by complaining about the police investigation and how he wanted it called off. Bligh said that this was nothing to do with him because it was a police, not a government matter.

So Ward, and we can imagine how desperate he was, threatened a bit of blackmail. He suggested that unless the investigation of his affairs was called off he would expose the real truth about Profumo and Keeler, which would cause the government considerable embarrassment. He said: 'I know myself that there is a great deal of potentially extremely explosive material in what I told you.'

He added for good measure that Profumo's statement was untrue, but would not elaborate. He left Admiralty House where the interview had taken place with a heavy heart. Even his remark that he had made a considerable sacrifice to protect Profumo had had no impact. He did not know that as soon as he left, arrangements were made to see Profumo to put the charge to him once again. Profumo stuck to his story and as the only opposition was Ward's statement (and we know what the government thought of him) nothing was done.

On 13 May Wilson wrote to Macmillan to ask what action was going to be taken over the information he had given him. Macmillan dismissed the request as if it was a bad smell. He said: 'There seems to be nothing in the papers which you sent which requires me to take further action.' How wrong he was!

On 19 May, Ward, realizing that the police were as hard at it as ever, took more action. He wrote to the Home Secretary and said:

It has come to my attention that the Marylebone police are questioning my patients and friends in a line, however tactful, which is extremely damaging to me both professionally and socially. This inquiry has been going on day after day for weeks.

The instruction to do this must come from the Home Office.

Over the past few weeks I have done what I could to shield Mr Profumo from his indiscretion, about which I complained to the security service at the time. When he made a statement in parliament I backed it up although I knew it to be untrue.

Possibly my efforts to conceal his part and to return to him a letter which Miss Keeler had sold to the *Sunday Pictorial* might make it appear that I had something to conceal myself. I have not.

The allegations which appear to be the cause of investigation, and which I only know through the line of questioning repeated to me, are malicious and entirely false. It is an invention of the press that Miss Keeler knew a lot of important people.

It was by accident that she met Mr Profumo and through Lord Astor that she met him again. I intend to take the blame no longer.

That I was against this liaison is a matter of record in the War Office.

Sir Godfrey Nicholson who has been a friend for twenty-five years is in possession of most of the facts since I consulted him at an early stage.

May I ask that the person who has lodged this false information against me be prosecuted.

There was no chance of the Home Secretary doing anything of the sort, even if he had known who had lodged the information (it was, of course, Lewis). An assistant sent back this reply: 'The Home Secretary has asked me to explain that the police, in making whatever inquiries they think proper, do not act under his direction.'

A few days later, on 20 May, Ward wrote to his MP, Sir Wavell Wakefield, to whom he suggested that an enquiry might be necessary 'when a minister has not told the truth to parliament'. The letter was passed on to the Chief Whip.

The same day he wrote to Wilson, saying: 'Obviously my efforts to conceal the fact that Mr Profumo had not told the truth in parliament have made it look as if I myself had something to hide. It is quite clear now that they must wish the facts to be known, and I shall see that they are.'

It was an unequivocal attempt to try to stop the police, a blackmail threat which was reasonable in the circumstances. Ward now knew without any doubt that the police had been given everything on a plate out of hate and malice. He knew Lewis was responsible and he did something about it, while Wilson, increasingly irritated by Macmillan's rudeness and laid-back attitude, sent him Ward's letter.

On 26 May Ward in desperation went to see Commander

Townsend to try to get him to call off his men, not knowing that Lewis had been there over five months earlier with his poison. It was, like his plea to the Home Secretary, a complete waste of time. No-one was going to do anything about it.

By this time Herbert and Burrows were well into their investigation and had arrested Rice-Davies at Heathrow on a minor motoring charge. She was brought before a court where she was remanded in custody for the sole reason that she might leave the country and she was a very important witness indeed. Ward knew this when he went to see the commander by appointment at Scotland Yard. We do not know exactly what was said at the meeting but the gist of it was in a letter Ward wrote to him after the meeting. It makes clear that he now realized what had been happening and who was responsible for it.

It was John Lewis. His malice was breath-taking and here was confirmation, if ever it was needed, as to the architect and prime mover in the Profumo affair, the wicked person who had started it moving and who had been aided by Profumo's lies and the row between Macmillan and the secret services. The letter which bared Ward's anguish read:

Dear Commander Townsend,

Thank you for the interview you gave me. I'm sure you can understand my feelings on this matter. From my point of view there is a situation where I am entitled to feel that the allegations made are false.

Although I have no knowledge of the precise charges I have a pretty good idea, from the questions reported back to me, what they add up to and yet the questioning goes on.

This implies one of two things – that you shall be 100 per cent certain that no influence or interference or pressure can be laid against the police, or that someone is really out to get me at any cost even on a charge that would later be found to have no substance. The making of such a charge would, as you know, be utterly ruinous to me. How I have survived up to now I do not know and it is probably due to the extreme loyalty of my friends.

There is also a great danger that newspapers offer money for specific information or for a certain type of story from irresponsible people. This was clear in the case of the Vassall landlady. I know that Mandy Rice-Davies has been offered money for a call-girl story and that she has offered such a story to

Time magazine and other newspapers. I also know that this was after the inquiries had started and was only to substantiate a story already in existence.

And then came the crux, the certain knowledge that it was all malice, and the name of the person who had started it. The only thing that Ward did not say was why Lewis should have done this. He could have said but he did not. Instead, he wrote: 'I am also entitled to feel that malice has been at work. Otherwise how could this thing have started? I know you would not have got this far without laid information. It must have been through parliament that Lewis has worked his own private malice.' Ward did not know that Lewis had worked his malice through the police as well. He went on: 'Everyone wanted me because he thought information would be useful. In the case of the Labour party it was to shop Mr Profumo and in the case of the press to revenge the imprisoned journalists. They accepted information in both cases. In both cases they failed to evaluate if the source was leaked for malice. This as I now know you will not fail to do.'

But what could the commander do? Lewis had been feeding him and his masters all the information necessary to investigate Ward. Lewis oozed malice as part of his character. Even if he had wanted, Townsend could do nothing now. The highest powers in the land were involved and the disaster could not be stopped.

Ward also mentioned another man using, he thought, malice. This was Laurence Bell, a 26-year-old salesman who was a tipster for the national newspapers. He picked up the line that Ward was a communist seeking nuclear information, that Keeler had slept with Profumo, and also that a junior minister might be up to no good with a friend, all of which he passed on when it was very much general knowledge. Bell, who liked to pose as a guard officer, was tried and acquitted in October 1963 for various indecency offences with guardsmen. He claimed that his arrest was a put-up job by the government to shut him up and keep him out of the way. He subpoenaed Labour MPs Emmanuel Shinwell and George Wigg. Wigg said he had once spoken to Bell, who told him things a few days before the matter was raised in the House of Commons in March that 'were more or less common knowledge' about the Profumo case. It was the kind of outrageous action in which Bell indulged – calling MPs as witnesses, dining with the guards at Windsor and in the Mall. He died from an overdose in April 1973, a self-styled 'cad of the century'. His marriage to an heiress had ended in divorce and he had gone downhill becoming a sad conman and a liar.

Ward went on in his letter: 'I am completely satisfied after I saw you that I am in no danger from the police in this respect since I know the truth myself. You will realize from my point of view that I also welcome the completion of the inquiry which I would like to be as full as possible.' He then repeated his offer at the interview that the commander should examine his finances and records, bank statements, appointment books and talk to his secretary and his solicitor who looked after his money. This offer was taken up the next day by Chief Inspector Herbert who went to see him. When Ward asked 'What exactly has been alleged against me? I believe it has been said that I procure young girls for men in high places,' Herbert said that procuration was amongst the allegations, which brought this outburst from Ward: 'It is ridiculous to say I have received money for introducing girls to men. Of course I always had pretty girls around me and took them to parties but if this is followed up by men and the men gave them presents surely there is no complaint against me and in any case I didn't see anything wrong in it.' This was his defence all the way through and he did not waver from it.

Ward's letter continued: 'There are innumerable friends and acquaintances whom you haven't got in touch with, whose names I can give you. You may search my flat. More than this I cannot suggest but in return I do beg you to look for malice behind all this and expose it for what it is.' No-one ever did.

He finished by saying that he had no complaint against the police and that their conduct had been tactful. It did him no good because the inquiry was not called off. But his shower of letters bore fruit in the Profumo direction. Questions were prepared to be asked for senior Labour statesmen in the House. They were directed to the Home Secretary, asking what information he had received from Ward about inquiries being carried out by the police. The questions were withdrawn after Wilson was given an appointment by Macmillan following the Ward letter to the Labour leader. The situations between the two politicians at this time was as follows:

On 25 April, following the 'a Mr Stephen Ward' sneer, Macmillan asked the security people to look into the matter. They sent a memo back, saying: 'We have no reason to suppose that Mr Profumo stands in need of further advice about security. There is no truth in the story that the security service was informed of the dates of, or anything else, in connection with Mr Profumo's alleged visits to Ward or to Miss Keeler.' Macmillan waited three weeks before writing back to Wilson to say 'I handed all the material to the appropriate authorities who studied it very carefully. There seems to be nothing in the papers you sent which requires me to take action.'

When the two met, Wilson said that he was disturbed to receive the Prime Minister's reply and that he thought Ward was a self-confessed Soviet intermediary and if the government were not prepared to take any action he would reserve the right to raise the matter in the House of Commons. Macmillan repeated that the security authorities had examined all the material and they were satisfied there were no unresolved security problems left over. He would ask them to have another look and advise him. George Wigg said that when Wilson left, Macmillan seemed even more casual than usual and was still unconvinced of any need for action. There was no problem. All was well.

But the meeting had an unusual sequel which brought matters to a head. The security staff received a minute about the meeting and had a look in their files. There was the statement that Keeler made on 26 January in which she told all. White quickly wrote a memo to Macmillan in which he said:

In a statement Christine Keeler made to the police in January 1963 she said that on one occasion, when she was going to meet Mr Profumo, Ward had asked her to discover from him the date on which certain atomic secrets were to be handed to West Germany by the Americans. It is understood that Miss Keeler denies ever having put such a question to Mr Profumo ... I am advised that the evidence would not be likely to support a successful prosecution of Ward under the Official Secrets Act. He is not known to us to have been in touch with any Russian since Ivanov's departure. The security risk that Ward represents seems to me to be slight.

Macmillan received the memo the same day and it must have wiped the complacent smile off his face. He acted very quickly indeed. His feelings were not dismay and shock because he still trusted his old colleague and was sure he had spoken the truth. But things were moving into a different realm – that of security.

It was 123 days after Keeler had told the police what had been going on that the statement finally arrived on the Prime Minister's desk, the desk of the head of security. In those four months the situation could have been saved, Profumo could have resigned gracefully when confronted with it. But the statement had stayed in the file of the security services.

The first thing that Macmillan did was to call the Lord Chancellor, Lord Dilhorne, the former Sir Reginald Manningham-Buller, and told him to undertake an inquiry at once. Secondly because the Whitsun recess was on them, he passed Wilson a note in the House in which he said;

> I have been thinking about our talk on Monday. I am sure in my own mind that the security aspect of the Ward case has been fully and efficiently watched but I think it is important that you should be in no doubt about it. I have therefore asked the Lord Chancellor to look carefully at the security reports and other documents which I have received in connection with this case and to make any inquiry which he deems necessary from the security authorities and the police and to advise me if, in his opinion, any further action is desirable.

Wilson scribbled a note back, asking Macmillan to announce this publicly. Macmillan did not do so on the grounds that he did not expect any further information to come from it. At the same time, there were whispered conversations going on between Profumo and Macmillan and then the Chief Whip at the back of the Speaker's chair.

Macmillan took a few days off in the Highlands (confident that all would be cleared up when he returned) leaving Butler in charge and Dilhorne making his inquiries. He told Profumo, who was going with his wife to Venice for a short holiday, that he would like to see him when he got back on Thursday 6 June. So fast did the Lord Chancellor do his work that he telegraphed Profumo via the War Office in Venice saying he would see him a day earlier.

Before he went, Profumo was seen separately by both the Chief Whip and the Prime Minister's Private Secretary Timothy

Bligh. They told him that it looked as though there would be an inquiry and, if there was a flaw in his story, it would do the government enormous damage. If he had said anything untrue he should confess now of his own accord. Profumo, for the last time, for the umpteenth time, lied: he stated that everything he had said was true.

But Profumo knew that this was the end, that he could not sustain his lie any longer. Over a candlelit dinner in Venice he told his wife the truth, the first time he had told anyone. She forgave him but said that they must come straight home. They did so by train to avoid the press who had seen them off at Heathrow and were back in London on Sunday 2 June. They drove down to Suffolk on Monday to see their friends, Mr and Mrs John Hare, (he was Minister of Agriculture and later Lord Blakenham). After a discussion they returned to London.

The next morning, 4 June, Profumo made an appointment to see Bligh at Admiralty House at half past nine. The Chief Whip was there too, perhaps having an inkling of what was to come.

There was no preamble. Profumo said straight out: 'I have to tell you that I did sleep with Miss Keeler and my statement in that respect was untrue.' It was indeed an admission and it instantly brought to an end his career (and that of the government a year later). He applied for the Chiltern Hundreds, the traditional way of resigning his seat, and later his name was removed from the list of privy councillors. He did not speak to Macmillan personally but hurried away into a private life of good works. His disgrace was complete. His shame was such that he did not hand his seals of office to the Queen. He sent them.

It was as well that he did not speak to Macmillan. The Prime Minister was hurt deeply by the betrayal and the broken trust. In his wildest dreams he could not believe anyone, least of all an old colleague, could lie to the House of Commons in a personal statement. He was very, very, genuinely upset.

There was the traditional exchange of letters, polite but cold – ice-cold, from Macmillan in reply:

Dear Prime Minister,
      You will recollect that on 22 March following certain allegations made in Parliament, I made a personal statement.
      At that time rumour had charged me with assisting in the disappearance of a witness and with being involved in some

possible breach of security. So serious were these charges that I allowed myself to think that my personal association with that witness, which had also been the subject of rumour, was, by comparison, of minor importance only. In my statement I said that there had been no impropriety in this association. To my very deep regret I have to admit that this was not true, and that I misled you, and my colleagues, and the House. I ask you to understand that I did this to protect, as I thought, my wife and family, who were equally misled, as were my professional advisers.

I have come to realize that, by this deception, I have been guilty of a grave misdemeanour and despite the fact that there is no truth whatever in the other charges, I cannot remain a member of your Administration, nor of the House of Commons.

I cannot tell you of my deep remorse for the embarrassment I have caused to you, to my colleagues in the Government, to my constituents and to the Party which I have served for the past twenty-five years.

Yours sincerely,
Jack Profumo

The Right Hon. Harold Macmillan, MP.

Dear Profumo,

The contents of your letter of 4 June have been communicated to me, and I have heard them with deep regret. This is a great tragedy for you, your family, and your friends. Nevertheless, I am sure you will understand that in the circumstances, I have no alternative but to advise The Queen to accept your resignation.

Yours very sincerely,
Harold Macmillan

The Right Hon. John Profumo, OBE, MP.

Both were unaware of the irony of the situation. Neither of them had met or were even aware of John Lewis, the architect of the disaster. He knew them by sight and reputation but no more than that. They were victims of his hatred for Stephen Ward, nothing more: his consuming obsession that dragged in outsiders for no other reason than that they had become caught in the chain of events, a chain of which they knew nothing.

16

THE END OF THE AFFAIR

While Macmillan prepared to fight for his political life and that of his government; while Profumo went to the East End where he rehabilitated himself in the eyes of royalty and his colleagues over the years and never explained nor wrote a word in his defence and while Ward was doing everything to stave off the irreparable harm Lewis had done him (and the government at the same time), Keeler was having problems in the witness box at the trial of Lucky Gordon.

She arrived for the trial on 5 June in a chauffuer-driven Rolls and posed for the cameras. She accused Gordon of hitting her, and he accused her in a great outburst, having dismissed his counsel, of telling lies. He said that he wanted two friends who he said were there to be called. The police tried to find them overnight but could not. One was in prison.

The jury were out for only ten minutes and they found Gordon guilty. It was his third conviction for violence in six years and the judge told him: 'You terrorized Miss Keeler over a period of time and she was very frightened of you.' That was true, but this time they had got the wrong man. Gordon was gaoled for three years and led away screaming his innocence.

The Profumo confession brought two opposite outbursts from his former close colleagues. One came from Iain Macleod, who said: 'I was, and am, a personal friend of Jack and Valerie Profumo and I think it is a tragedy that this should have happened.'

The other, dramatic and angry in its delivery, came from Lord Hailsham, later to be Lord Chancellor. He roared on television: 'A great party is not to be brought down because of the scandal of a woman of easy virtue and a proved liar,' which echoed the words of his party leader to close friends: 'I will not be brought down by a tart.'

Meanwhile, on 7 June, the Director of Public Prosecutions held a conference with the police and his legal advisers. The decision was taken that there was enough evidence to prosecute Ward.

On that afternoon a journalist friend of Ward's, whose paper was negotiating to buy his story, went to see Commander Townsend. The friend said that Ward wanted to get away for a while, possibly to the United States, and asked if there would be any objections.

None at all, said the commander, friend of Lewis, listener to Ward's troubles, just a few formalities such as signing a form or two and then off he could go.

It was not to be. Townsend told his officers that Ward was about to leave the country and the next morning they went to arrest him, just as his journalist friend was telling him that everything was all right.

Poor Ward! Gentleman to the last, keeper of the public schoolboys' code, he asked the arresting policeman if they would mind going a little way from the house at Watford where he was spending the weekend to avoid embarrassing his host. He walked down a country lane in open-neck shirt, slacks, dark glasses and carpet slippers and went quietly. It was, not that he knew it, the end of his life.

He appeared in court on the Monday, the day after the first instalment in the *News of the World* of Keeler's story of her affair with Profumo, for which it had paid her £23,000. On the same day the *Sunday Mirror* had published the 'Darling' letter, for which it had paid £200 an age before. He spent the weekend in the cells and was remanded in custody where he stayed for several weeks until finally he was given £3,000 bail until his trial on 23 July. He walked out to freedom for the last time on 3 July.

But this time the country had gone into a fit. The disclosures of immorality in high places, of sex orgies at country houses, of fornicating, four in a bed and all the other activities which the participants had enjoyed so much and over which the public drooled jealously at breakfast on Sunday, had brought out British hypocrisy at its very worst. There were genuine tut-tuts that such things should go on in high places from *The Times* and other serious newspapers, but the general tone was the typically

British one of saying how disgusting and awful it was, with a lingering longing that if they had not actually been there, they would have liked to have known it was going on so that they could have had the choice.

Macmillan was to cite the Victorian essayist Macaulay to support his view of moral recrimination when he wrote: 'We know of no spectacle so ridiculous as the British public in one of its periodical fits of morality.' Macmillan may have thought this but the country turned against him and his government, shocked that such behaviour was going on, whether their views were genuine or not. The stock market fell, Labour had its biggest lead in the polls for years (one they sustained right through to victory the next year) and there were considerable fears that the government would fall there and then and that Macmillan would have to go. His future hung on a gossamer thread for days but he survived the cabinet meeting (for which the Home Secretary was brought back by warship from Guernsey) on the grounds of Tory unity. He then had to face parliament with the full guns of Wilson and Wigg blasting him.

Looking back, it is difficult to see what all the fuss was about. The security danger, if there ever was one, had vanished almost two years before when Profumo stopped sleeping with Keeler. Ward's activities, for what they were worth, had been stopped by his arrest. All the ingredients that were now causing the tearing of sackcloth, and the wailing and shouting, the pontificating and sermonizing as everyone denied knowing Keeler (however much they may have known her or wanted to know her to take her to bed) had long gone.

The facts that caused uproar amongst the sanctimonious public were that a senior minister had done the unforgivable and lied to the Commons in a personal statement; that he had been found out for having an affair with a little poppet with lovely long legs and gorgeous hair and body (which was why so many were cross); that it had taken nearly two years for him to be found out; and that when he had admitted it, a whole series of stories in the papers had uncovered a hornets' nest of ecstasy and orgy.

Mcmillan put it into perspective ten years on when he gave a BBC interview. He was talking about the difference of standards in public and private life. There is no doubt that what Profumo did hurt him greatly. It was a genuine hurt, not an actor-manager protestation of hurt or sham emotion of which he was sometimes accused. He told the interviewer on television:

> Nobody has any right to enquire into the private life of ordinary
> citizens and subjects, it's their affair. They're not imposing
> themselves on you.
>
> But if you go into public life, become Prime Minister, become
> a Foreign Secretary, become a member of Cabinet, nobody
> asked you to, nobody asked you to stand for Parliament, nobody
> asked you to carry the burdens I describe here.
>
> You have to be careful about complaining about them. There
> are plenty of people who will take them from you. But you do set
> yourself up to do something different to other people. And to
> take the very great responsibility, moral responsibility of coming
> into a position of leadership. And I think that does imply certain
> parallel duties. You owe it if you step into the front-line and if
> you can use a very reactionary, an old-fashioned sentence which
> hasn't done much harm to our country through many centuries,
> you should behave like an officer and a gentleman.

That was the nub of it: the lie.

But on the weekend when it all broke ten years before Macmillan was not nearly so sanguine. He was staying at Gleneagles
for a weekend's golf with his wife and had the Sunday papers to
digest at breakfast. He must have had dyspepsia afterwards. He
said at a reception: 'They may call me a twister but I don't do the
twist,' as a joke. Later he was to have strangers hissing insults into
his ears at the traditional garden parties. It was a mad period and
people said things they would now regret. There were marvellous
cartoons in the papers, including one from Giles showing an old
Tory lady, pearls swinging, running beside her equally aged
husband who is racing for the phone. She is demanding why, if he
does not know Christmas Keeler, he should be in such a hurry to
get to the phone.

On a personal note, I remember going to John Hare's home
as a reporter to ask him about the car he lent to Profumo, not
knowing it was to be used for an assignation. As I drove down
the long drive of his home near Ipswich I saw this figure with a
leg in plaster look towards me, rise on stick and run-hobble into
his house. It was the minister. The panic was infectious.

The Tories were becoming more and more anxious. In the
shires, the coldbed of morals, the feeling was one of dismay and
disgust. The people had to be won round. The work was done by
senior Tory figures such as Lord Poole and Macleod, joint

chairmen of the party. They were fighting for survival. No-one wants to be in Opposition. The two sensed that party workers and officials outside London were not with them. It was a tricky time but the shires were finally won after the big debate, chosen because the Labour party had the luck to pick the motion when the House resumed after the recess. They would debate Profumo, but it would be on security only.

The Times insisted in a leader: 'It is a moral issue' and broke the story of a split in Cabinet over Macmillan's leadership. On the eve of the great debate there was a very strong chance that the government might be defeated by some of its own MPs, and for once it was not just the regular dissenters who might vote against their own party, so strong were feelings on the matter. Macmillan was very worried.

No debate had attracted such attention for years as the one that was held on 17 June. The place was packed. Lord Hailsham had insisted that a three-line Whip meant attendance, not voting for the party. Several MPs, not normally the type to rebel, were to take him at his word, notably the elegant Nigel Birch.

The galleries were full, some with women dressed almost for the Ascot meeting three weeks ahead. The man responsible for everyone else being there, John Lewis, was present too. He did not boast about what he had done. He was just delighted that he had achieved so much for the Labour party (although they were never to recognize the fact in any way at all) and was almost in sight of seeing the total come-uppance of his enemy.

The debate started at 3.33 p.m. and the vote was taken over six hours later. Labour had instructed its members to stay silent while Macmillan spoke, a speech that would salvage or wreck his parliamentary career.

Wilson started savagely but without any of the histrionics which were to become his mark. He was a brilliant speaker and debater at any time. This time he scored his points with a well-prepared speech.

He started thus: 'This is a debate without precedent in the annals of the house. It arises from disclosures which have shocked the moral conscience of the nation. There is clear evidence of a sordid underworld network, the extent of which cannot yet be measured and which we cannot debate today because of proceedings elsewhere.' He meant the forthcoming trial of Stephen Ward. Wilson went on:

There is the personal and family tragedy of one lately our colleague here. However much we condemn him, and we must condemn him, this is not the issue today.

What does concern us directly is that the late Secretary of State for War, faced with rumours and innuendo that could not be ignored, chose deliberately to lie to this House and in circumstances in which this House allows freedom of personal statement wthout question or debate on the premise that what is said is said in good faith.

It was a point to be re-iterated several times in the debate that followed, the only reason why Profumo was not allowed to return to public life. People still dismiss his lie as something anyone might do in the circumstances. It is not the fact that he lied that made it so bad, but that he abused the place, the occasion and the privilege that afforded him unquestionable right.

Wilson went on to say that what concerned Labour was whether any other minister connived or failed in his duty to ascertain the truth. And he added:

> What concerns us, too, is whether a man in a high position of trust, privy to the most secret information available to a government, through a continuing association with this squalid network imperilled our national security or created conditions in which a continuing risk to our security was allowed to remain.
>
> We are not here as a court of morals, although the nation as a whole cannot escape the responsibility so to act. But questions affecting national security and the duty of ministers of this House, must be pressed and probed today.
>
> This debate in one form or another must continue until the truth is known so far as it can ever be known.

Wilson was speaking twenty-three months after Profumo had met Keeler, twenty-two months after he had been warned about the link between Ward and Ivanov, twenty-two months after Profumo had been warned off and stopped sleeping with Keeler, six months after Ivanov had left the country. Was it really necessary? It does not appear so now but at the time the panic and hysteria in the country were a sight to behold and gave the rest of the world plenty of amusement.

Wilson that day was in his stride, reading from a prepared speech. He said:

Much has been known to members and the press for many months. Already in February the rumours were so pervasive and so widely canvassed in the press that there was a danger of widespread cynicism developing about Britain's national life, about the government and the House. It was none the less damaging because of the inability of the press through fear of libel action to publish these facts.

No such legal inhibitions stopped publication abroad. He claimed that two months ago salacious and damaging stories were appearing abroad, which was not in fact so. His point about the British press, however, was quite right. Normally timid, they were now terrified by what had happened to the *Daily Telegraph* and the *Daily Mail* when Lewis sued them over what was really a mild libel. Damages of £217,000 in 1961 would be in the millions now, a sum to stop any editor in his tracks. If Lewis was awarded that sum for a small libel, even though there was to be a retrial, what would a jury award a minister of the Crown if they said that he had had an affair with a call-girl and had shared her with a Russian spy? The mere thought stopped the heart.

After his vicious opening, Wilson proceeded to put the boot in point by point. It was a catalogue of accusation – that there had been slackness, inefficiency, perhaps deliberate inefficiency, too casual an approach – and he wanted answers.

During his speech he made a particularly telling and savage point when speaking of how well Keeler was faring in the commercial world. He said: 'There is something utterly nauseating about a system of society which pays a harlot twenty-five times as much as it pays its Prime Minister, 250 times as much as it pays its members of parliament and 500 times as much as it pays some of its ministers of religion.'

He spoke for well over an hour and then Macmillan, the old artist and actor, stood up to try to save his reputation and his skin. The whole tone of his speech was one of regret, of being let down by an old friend, and of sadness that the security forces of which he was head had not kept him properly informed. It brought cries at one stage of: 'Nobody tells me nuffing.'

He started in low key. He said sadly:

As Mr Wilson has observed, this debate is taking place in conditions wholly unprecedented. A great shock has been given to parliament and indeed to the whole country.

To me, as head of the administration what has happened has inflicted a deep, bitter and lasting wound. I do not remember in the whole of my life or even in the political history of the past, a case of a minister of the Crown who has told a deliberate lie to his wife, his legal advisers, his ministerial colleagues, not once but over and over again, who has repeated this lie to the House of Commons as a personal statement, which as Mr Wilson reminded us, implies it is privileged and who has subsequently taken legal action and recovered damages on the basis of falsehood.

This is almost unbelievable but it is true.

He said he had gone away believing Profumo, but on the last day of his Scottish holiday he learned that his old colleague had indeed lied. Macmillan went on:

> Since we cannot, I fear, put much confidence in anything he has said, the problem of security is enhanced but in addition moral issues of the deepest kind are involved.
>
> For what greater moral crime can there be than to deceive those naturally inclined to trust you, those who have worked with you, served with you and are your colleagues?
>
> In a period of ministerial office which amounts altogether to seventeen years more especially in the last six years as Prime Minister, I have had to face, like all ministers, grave and baffling difficulties.
>
> This is different and I find it difficult to tell the House what a blow it has been to me for it seems to have underminded one of the very foundations upon which political life must be conducted.

Macmillan went on to deny that he had ever misled anyone, saying that he had not been given information at any times other than those he stated. He was not his usual self at all. The stuffing and zest seemed to have gone and there was none of his effortless, casual, throw-away lines. But he was convincing.

He dwelt for some time on the meeting of the ministers the night they drafted Profumo's statement. They accepted his word because he had told the story so many times. They accepted that the letter, the 'Darling' letter, contained nothing – 'I do not live among young people' – to concern anyone. They accepted the word of a colleague, that he would not tell a lie if in the long run he would be exposed.

Macmillian explained: 'I could not believe that a man would be so foolish, even if so wicked, not only to his colleagues in the House but be prepared to issue a writ in respect of libel which he must know to be true. Any doubts I may have had were removed.' That was why he went down to the House to be beside Profumo when he made his lying personal statement. Macmillan also wanted the country to know that at no time did he have any indication from the police or security forces that there was any reason to doubt Profumo's statement about his connection with Ward and his short friendship with Keeler. He then tried the please-feel-sorry-for-me approach:

In recent days I have been trying to search my heart and conscience and have approached the matter in this way: there is the question of justice and there is the question of good judgment. I know I have acted honourably, I believe I have acted justly. And I hope when they have heard my account members will consider that I have acted with proper diligence and prudence.

He tried the blame-the-security services tack:

In view of the discussions between my office and the security services at the beginning of February and as things have turned out I think it very unfortunate that this information was not given to me.

But finally he gave the I-throw-myself-on-your mercy ending:

I said at the beginning it was my duty to act honourably, to act justly and to act prudently. My colleagues have been deceived and I have been deceived, grossly deceived. The House has been deceived. But we have not been parties to deception and I claim, upon a fair view of the facts as I have set them out, that I am entitled to the sympathetic understanding and confidence of the House and the country.

It was to be enough. When the vote was taken at a minute before ten the Tory majority was sixty-nine although whether Macmillan would survive the party conference in Blackpool in October was another matter. There were twenty-seven abstentions, a high figure but not nearly as bad as the Whips first feared. No-one was going to commit suicide.

Macmillan had to wait a long time before he was sure of his victory. He had to listen to two speeches, both extremely hard-hitting, both in different styles. The first came from Nigel Birch and the second from Wigg, who had waited a long time for the opportunity to have his say. Birch said in his most cutting style that the real issue was whether it was right to accept Profumo's personal statement because Profumo had never struck him as at all like a cloistered monk and Keeler was a professional prostitute. He said: 'He was not a man who was ever likely to tell the absolute truth in a tight corner and at the time the statement was made he was in a very tight corner indeed.' Birch's view was that Macmillan genuinely believed Profumo and for that reason the Prime Minister should be acquitted of any sort of dishonour. But he continued:

> On the other hand, on the question of competence and good sense I cannot think that the verdict can be favourable.
>
> What is to happen now? I cannot myself see at all that we can go on acting as nothing has happened. We cannot just have business as usual. I myself feel that the time will come very soon when my Right Hon. friend ought to make way for a much younger colleague. I feel that ought to happen.
>
> I certainly will not quote at him the savage words of Cromwell, (They are: 'It is not fit that you should sit here any longer ... you shall now give place to better men') but perhaps some of the words of Browning might be appropriate, in his poem 'The Lost Leader.'
>
> The last line is: 'Never glad confident morning again!' So I hope that the change will not be too long delayed.

Wigg was never a witty, thrusting speaker. He knew his subject, researched every point of his speech and then made it. But this time he had had enough. He did not think much of Profumo, as we know, but he thought even less of Lord Hailsham and his attack on him was astonishing. He had a go at Profumo and his job record too but but he knew that Labour had already made the point and had the Tories on the run. He was right. For a week after the debate there was panic, real panic, calls for Macmillan's head on a platter, cries of anguish and woe, hysteria, and in the shires and sticks there was pandemonium. Macmillan was to steady it but the feeling ran on and with so many marginal seats in their grasp Wilson and his men were very confident about the outcome of the 1964 election. They needed to thank Lewis and Wigg for that, and Wigg took advantage of the occasion.

He started by criticizing Hailsham over his television outburst, saying that if he saw both on either side of the road he would go to the sinner Profumo rather than a sinister saint of Hailsham's type. Having got that off his chest he rounded on Profumo, his lack of success as War Minister and how he had lowered Army standards.

Wigg went through the record of his inquiries into the Profumo Affair and declared: 'The mistake which Profumo made, his only mistake, was the one which is unforgivable to the party opposite: he did not get away with it, he got found out.' He finished by calling on Macmillan to resign, and his whole administration with him.

Wigg's job was done. He sat down a satisfied man as he had a right to be. There only remained his evidence to Lord Denning to give, for Wigg, as we know, was not a vindictive man once honour was satisfied. The smears that he and his colleagues had used their privilege to bring the matter out into the open had been withdrawn and the accusations that had been brought forward in the interests of security by Labour justified and acknowledged. That was enough and he left it as it was.

Not so Lewis. There was much more to come – sweet, sweet revenge when Ward came up for trial. Lewis had high expectations that Ward would be found guilty on the evidence that Commander Townsend and his men had uncovered with their persistence. Never in his wildest dreams, and Lewis had some wild dreams, did he imagine what would happen.

17

VICTORY FOR LEWIS

The trial started on Monday 21 July, in much the same atmosphere as the guillotining in the French Revolution. The crowds queued in their best clothes to get a glimpse of the actors in the farce that was played out below them. They were hampered because they could not see the faces of the witnesses in the box and they could see only the back of Dr Ward as he sketched away for most of the eight-day trial. It was only when the weight of the evidence and the judge's summing up hit him in the solar plexus that he put down his pad.

In the weeks between his arrest and the fall of Profumo, the fortunes of the Tory party had not risen at all. The president of the United States had paid a visit to Macmillan and confided in him that he got a headache if he did not have sex at least once a day. Macmillan, who had asked Lord Denning to investigate the fall of Profumo and whether there had been a security lapse and what could be learnt from it, did not reply. What could he say, when his wife had been having sex as often as possible with one of his best friends (Bob Boothby) for years?

Macmillan had written to the Queen, telling her of his distress at what had occurred and talking of these 'very disturbing affairs'. The former Master of the Rolls made a thorough investigation, taking statements from 160 people including Macmillan, Profumo, Ward and Keeler within forty-nine days and wrote the report so that it came out in September. It was an unprecedented inquiry because there was no machinery to deal with the moral misbehaviour of a minister.

Macmillan went on television but was not convincing and his stock fell further when Heath announced that Philby was definitely the Third Man. There was an ironic note at the start of the Ward trial. He had an exhibition of his sketches on show in Bloomsbury, in the west end of London, and it was obviously popular not only because the sketches were good but because of Ward's notoriety. Among the sketches were eleven of the royal family, all for sale because the money was needed to help pay Ward's legal costs. But as the trial proceeded and the evidence became quite startling in its sexual frankness, someone decided the royals most certainly must not be associated with the name of Ward. The Fourth Man, Sir Anthony Blunt, homosexual, spy and lifelong traitor, was asked by some loyal subject still unknown to take a suitcase stuffed with £5,000 in notes down to the gallery and buy the drawings. The silver-haired adviser on pictures to the Queen walked in, paid cash and departed with the sketches, which were never to be seen again. The next year Blunt, who joined the Communists with Burgess, Maclean and Philby at Trinity College, Cambridge, in the mid-thirties, was finally uncovered as a traitor. Like his homosexual friend Burgess he admitted it. It was not until 1979 that it was thought fit to tell the public because Blunt had been given immunity for confessing. He was stripped of his knighthood when it did become a matter of public knowledge and he died of a heart attack in 1983.

When the trial opened Ward pleaded not guilty to five charges. There were three charges that he lived partly or wholly off the earnings of prostitution, two involving Keeler and Rice-Davies, and two of procuring girls under twenty-one to have sex with a third party.

Some who were present at the trial say it was a put-up job, and that although the summing up by the judge, Mr Justice Marshall, a Pickwickian character without fun, a pompous, small man known as the Hen, reads fairly to both prosecution and defence, it was the tone in which it was delivered, the valleys and peaks, the softly barbed way in which he sneered at the defence, that turned the jury.

I was not there but I do remember my anger that Ward should have been convicted on such flimsy evidence as I read about it in the papers every day. It was, of course, the jury who convicted him but they must have taken leave of their senses: were they such smug moralists and hypocrites that they could not see that they were being used by the government to witch-hunt poor old Stephen Ward?

But now, nearly thirty years later and re-reading the evidence, there was a lot for the jury to think about. The revelations must have been quite horrific, tales of a man of fifty picking women off the streets, taking them back to his flat, screwing them and then sketching them over coffee afterwards; of Ward picking an elfin whore off the road late at night, taking her home and telling her to strip and go into the bedroom where she had sex with a man, and then coming back time after time to cane and even horsewhip naked men while she wore (for Ward) exciting, shiny, high-heeled shoes and sexy underwear. The girl was from Birmingham, twenty years old and tiny, eyes dulled as she stood in her green raincoat and white silk scarf to give evidence in answer to Mr Mervyn Griffith-Jones, an Edwardian-style barrister, who spoke in the language of the nineteenth century and regarded Ward – in his words – as a thoroughly filthy, wicked fellow.

Almost choking on the words, the barrister, (who had asked in the *Lady Chatterley's Lover* trial two years before if it was a book which you would allow your servant to read) asked: 'With your knowledge of the trade, rather profession, what would be the normal payment for services that you rendered? How much a time?'

'£5.'

'And the whipping, how much a stroke?'

'£1 a stroke.'

Her evidence was described by Ward as a tissue of lies. At one time the parade of prostitutes became too much for him and he cried out in anguish: 'Anyone who comes in from the street and comes forward into this court can come in and say I am lying. In a general atmosphere of villainy surrounding this case almost anyone comes forward and makes suggestions. Apart from this case I am considered to be a truthful person.'

The jury heard Keeler say that she had slept with Profumo among others but she was not a prostitute and never had been. The judge totted up the number of men that Keeler and Rice-Davies had slept with. Rice-Davies included Charles Clore, Emil Savundra (whose names were not spelt out in court) and Douglas Fairbanks and Bill Astor (whose names were given in full). Rice-Davies, who won much admiration for her could-not-care-less attitude in front of all these old-fashioned men in funny clothes, said that she named Fairbanks because she did not like him and when challenged that Astor said he had not slept with her, said: 'Well, he would, wouldn't he?'

It became plain that if all the activities alleged were going on in Ward's flat, particularly when the Profumo rumour broke and afterwards, there must have been dozens of witnesses, for, as Ward said, there were sometimes so many people (and these, although it was not stated, included Lewis's spies) that he had difficulty in getting in himself. The jury also heard that Keeler and Rice-Davies, far from providing Ward with a living, and he made a very good living as one of the top osteopaths in London anyway, owed him money for rent and food and to repay other loans he had given them.

I think the problem the jury had was that they were not only in the strange world of the Old Bailey, amongst the antiquated customs of the judicial system, but that they were hearing of a world of orgy and fornication that was even more strange to them. It must have amazed them to learn that the little whore could cane to her heart's content and give the money to Ward but that was not living off the proceeds of prostitution because only normal sex counted for that. However much Ward denied it, they could not put it out of their minds.

And they had another problem, which was how to define a prostitute? The prosecutor forgot that he was in the nineteenth century for a while and that sex was something only the lesser breeds do, to say: 'A prostitute is not necessarily the kind of woman that one pictures when one uses that word. It is not necessary for her to ply her trade on the street corner, or, as is perhaps more customary since a recent Act [Wolfenden], to set herself up as a call-girl and make herself available when telephoned. Prostitution is a matter of law and, for the purposes of this case, is where a woman offers her body for sexual intercourse or any acts of lewdness for money.'

Ward put it a different way. He said during his evidence: 'My attitude has been that if a girl wanted it and I was willing to have sexual intercourse I would urge myself to. I would never force anyone to do it.' His view was that prostitution was where there was no feeling between the two people and there was always feeling when Keeler and Rice-Davies slept with men.

His friends never told the court how they felt about it. They abandoned him almost totally, apart from an international sculptor. Ward's desertion by his friends brought this comment from the judge: 'There may be many reasons why he has been abandoned in his extremity. You must not guess at them, but this is clear: if Stephen Ward was telling the truth in the witness box there are in this city many witnesses of high estate and low who could have come and testified support of his evidence.' They did not, not even the mysterious Mr Woods of MI5 from Room 393 in the War Office for whom Ward worked.

The judge, when summing up, put his view of prostitution. He said: 'I think, that a person may fairly be said to be living on the earnings of prostitution if he is paid by prostitutes for goods and services supplied by him to them for the purpose of their prostitution which they would not be supplied with but for the fact that they were prostitutes.'

He said there were four things the law required to be proved before they could convict Ward. They were: firstly, that he knowingly assisted prostitutes to ply their trade, that what he supplied was for their trade, that he would not have done this unless they were trading as prostitutes, and finally that he received payment out of their earnings for that assistance.

James Burge, who defended Ward brilliantly, opened his case to the jury by talking about the background to the case – the fact that they all knew what it was about because there had been so much in the press and how that affected the charge of living off the earnings of prostitution.

He suggested that they might be thinking that there was no answer to the charges, that 'Ward was a filthy man who had been living upon the earnings of women for years and procuring for people in high places.' But, he said, the jury should look at Ward's life as a whole. Since the House of Commons declaration in March, 'the police have combed the country in a frenzy in order to find evidence implicating the accused,' he said. 'You have heard of the number of witnesses that have been interviewed and you have seen some of them, and you have heard the circumstances and places in which they were interviewed.'

But the case had cut the evidence to its true proportions, which were quite different. He asked the jury to consider Ward's double life, and not just think because of the pre-trial publicity, that he was a procurer who lived off the earnings of prostitution. He then gave a sharp portrait of Ward. He said:

When he comes to give his evidence and call his witnesses you will hear of the two lives of Stephen Ward. You will hear first, and this is accepted [by the judge and prosecution] that he is a skilled and successful osteopath earning substantial sums of money.

And you will hear of his second life, and a life that may not appeal to you and quite clearly does not appeal to many people, that of a bohemian, a man who is a talented artist and who will not flinch from telling you that he is very highly sexed and indeed has had affairs with a great many women.

He lives alone and an artist's life consisted of gay parties and attractive girls, drawing them and making love.

The prosecution of course suggest that he has a third life, that of a parasite, living upon the immoral earnings of prostitution and in fact procuring women for that purpose.

You are not concerned I hope – because if you are we might as well plead guilty – with the standards of moral conduct of this man.

That is far short, and the accused will be forced to admit it, of anything you will approve of. But that does not mean because you have a low standard of moral conduct – because you might be considered depraved or a loose liver – that you have committed the criminal offence and perhaps the most loathsome criminal offence of a man who lives not on his own work but on some prostitute upon whom he battens in order to keep him.

He added a little more, partly pointed, although he did not say so and (unless Ward had told him) he did not know, at John Lewis:

Although public opinion has obviously been horrified by the scandal that was raised through no fault of this man [and how Lewis must have loved that, guilty but unknown] and therefore demands expiation, some speedy sacrifice so that the matter can be established and disposed of and forgotten, that is not a consideration that will affect you in deciding the issue here.

Looking at it, as its closest, accepting the fact that this man is an artist, who lives with a number of women, sleeps with them, behaving perhaps outrageously, can you say he was a man really living on immoral, earnings in the first place or has it been established that he is a procurer?

Of course the jury could, certainly when it came to living on immoral earnings. No juryman after that summer of non-stop publicity, generated since Lewis had heard Keeler's tale, could close his eyes and ears to what he could read or hear. It is a flaw in the legal system that anyone should expect a jury to put out of their minds what they know.

But the judge persisted in the fantasy when he began his summing up, initially when one reads it – and it was the view of those there – perfectly fairly. He said:

> We are now reaching the last stages of a trial that has probably achieved greater notoriety than any trial in recent years.
>
> There have been, as we all know repercussions arising out of what we have to investigate which have widely spread their tentacles across the public life of this country and have aroused great interest in foreign countries.
>
> One would have thought from what we have all been faced with in the national newspapers that this country has become a sort of sink of iniquity. But you and I know that the even tenor of family life over the overwhelming majority of our population goes quietly and decently on.
>
> One of the facts that has resulted from this kind of background is that a great power, sometimes described as the fourth estate, has power to give false emphasis to this fact and present distorted pictures.
>
> I just referred to this for the sole reason that I want us, if we can, to consider this case in an atmosphere that has put aside many of the considerations that have inevitably obtruded themselves on our attention now for many weeks.
>
> This is an important case and I hope we can come properly to any decision which has to be made. It is an important case to the public because if activities of the kind that are laid against the accused are taking place in the heart of this great metropolis, surely it is of real national interest that it shall be unravelled, properly assessed and if established, dealt with.
>
> Here is a man of hitherto good character; by that is meant in this trial hitherto of previous conviction. You will have to assess the value of that aspect of the evidence in a way that I have never been called upon to assess before.
>
> When a man says he is of good character when charged with a sexual offence, albeit he says at the same time 'I am an immoral man', it is one of your tasks to assess in those circumstances how character shall in fact operate.
>
> To engage in activities so repellent to most people is, according to his own account, to sink very low. We have a duty to clear our minds of prejudice so that prejudice, the great enemy of true justice will not bend and warp our judgment.

Later, in putting the case for the prosecution and then that of the defence, the judge's manner suggested that he did not approve of Ward and those who were present say that it was this that influenced the jury. Who can say all these years on, when folklore has added to the story? But it is certain that Ward left the court that evening believing that he was finished.

He could not have been happy about the result of the Lucky Gordon appeal. Gordon was freed because the police had found the two missing West Indian witnesses and taken statements from them. They also had a tape recording that Keeler had made when telling her story ready for its sale, in which she told who had really hit her (an English acquaintance) and how the two witnesses, who were both terrified of the police because of their past, had hidden in a bedroom. It had been handed to Wigg soon to become Paymaster General (known as Spymaster General) as reward for his service in the Profumo Affair and to Harold Wilson, who had passed it on to the police.

But in the Court of Appeal that fine July day the Lord Chief Justice, Lord Parker, ruled that if the evidence of the two men had been put before the jury at the Gordon trial it might have caused a doubt. Without saying what was in the statements, he and his colleagues (including the judge who tried the Lewis divorce, Mr Justice Sachs) allowed the appeal without hearing any more.

Lord Parker neglected to say one thing that might have affected the Ward trial. He could have said that Gordon was going free because the two men in their statement made it quite clear that Keeler had lied. He did not say this, and if he had it might have influenced the Ward jury's view of Keeler's words. But Lord Parker said he would like to make it clear that the court was not holding that Keeler's evidence was untruthful. He said: 'She might well have been speaking the truth, but at the same time if this further evidence might, as the court thought it might, have raised a doubt in the jury's mind, then this was the only course open to this court.'

Down at the Old Bailey his decision, that they were not questioning Keeler's veracity as a truthful witness, was relayed to the jury by the prosecutor and the judge. No-one knows what the jury thought, but it could only have hardened their belief that Keeler was telling the truth.

Mr Griffith-Jones said:

As I understand from the note I have, the Lord Chief Justice said that it might be that Miss Keeler's evidence was completely truthful but in view of the fact that there were witnesses now available who were not available at the trial it was felt that the court could not necessarily say that the jury in that case would have returned the same verdict as they did if the two witnesses had been called.

That is all it amounts to. The Court of Criminal Appeal has not found whether Miss Keeler was telling the truth, they have allowed the appeal simply and solely because the two witnesses were not there.

Finally, if you convict in this case and should there be anything in the Gordon case of which you do not know which has turned up in this appeal it will afford this defendant grounds of appeal thereafter to the same court which has decided the Gordon appeal this morning and that court will be in possession of all the facts so that no injustice, you may think, can have been done.

Poor Ward. He probably knew these facts which could prove that Keeler had lied and should he be convicted, he might use them in his appeal. It may have been, however, that he was not thinking that way. He was waiting for the judge to sum up. But first, the judge had a few words to say on the appeal.

His view was that the Court of Appeal, and he understood their workings because he had been sitting there, had considered that the two missing witnesses had been found in this case ('an offence of violence of some kind against Miss Christine Keeler,' he said) and had made statements and if these had been available to the jury they might not have convicted.

He explained:

The decision of the court, therefore, you must take to mean involves no assessment of the evidence of Miss Christine Keeler and it has come to no decision upon it.

It only confirms what I have already told you – that this is one of those extraneous matters which I have asked you to exclude from your minds but I thought it right to tell you the grounds upon which that decision has been found so that you may feel at least that I have taken you completely into my confidence and have been completely frank about it.

It was not an extraneous matter. It was a vital matter. If the

Court of Appeal had know of all the facts, that Keeler had deliberately lied about the two witnesses and who it was that attacked her, who can say what the Ward jury would have done?

But they did not know.

And then Ward went and spoilt it all by taking a massive overdose of Nembutal. He went to the flat where he was staying, chatted to friends, journalists, his current girl-friend, his host, an official from Lord Denning's office about the evidence of two girls, all quite normally, wrote seventeen farewell letters to friends and officials, and then took a lethal 35 mg dose of the sleeping pills.

That was in the early hours of 1 August, the day the judge was to finish his summing up and the jury to retire. When he heard the news, the judge promptly and with the full pomposity of the law which looked an ass because he did so, withdrew bail and ordered a bedside guard for Ward. He continued summing up and the jury retired, letting Ward fade quietly away with no interest in living, in Ward 3D at St Stephen's hospital. It was not far from the flat in Mallard Street in central London where his host found him when he did not answer the phone ringing beside him in the morning. The comatosed man was carried out on a stretcher under a blanket with the press photographers in attendance.

Those who hoped to see Ward sent down for a swingeing sentence – and the judge had the power to make it seven years, the maximum for living off immoral earnings – hoped for his recovery, so that he could stand in the dock again and get his judicial come-uppance for causing so much trouble in high places. Those who were ashamed at what was going on in their name, having a sneaking feeling that things were not quite right, hoped for his death and release from the indignity and humiliation he would have to face. Most were indifferent, thinking, if they thought at all, that he had had a fair trial because everyone gets a fair trial under British justice.

Lewis was astonished. He had hoped that Ward would be convicted and end in gaol. Then he could drool with revenge at the thought of the sexy osteopath, friend of top people and royalty, slopping out with common criminals and the scum of society. But now it was not like that. Ward was hanging between life and death. Lewis, like everyone else, could only wait and see.

One of the letters Ward wrote before he took his pills was to the friend who was his host. It read:

> I am sorry I had to do this here. It's really more than I can stand
> – the horror day after day at the court and in the streets. It's not
> only fear – it's a wish not to let them get me. I'd rather get myself
> …
> I do hope I haven't let people down too much. I tried to do my
> stuff but after Marshall's summing up I'd given up all hope.
> I'm sorry to disappoint the vultures. I only hope this has done
> the job. Delay resuscitation as long as possible.'

It was a reasonable request because he had lost everything. His friend however instinctively rang for help as soon as he found Ward.

The leading vulture was Lewis. He, like everyone else, waited for the verdict and when it came after the jury had been out for four hours and thirty-five minutes it was not quite what was expected. They found him not guilty of the third charge of living off immoral earnings of street girls and of the charges of procuring girls but they did find him guilty of living off the immoral earnings of Keeler and Rice-Davies, both of whom had said that they owed him more money than they had ever given him.

The judge never had the chance to put Ward away, for he died two days later, at 3.45 p.m. on 3 August, without regaining consciousness. The policeman at his bedside to make sure he did not escape was not needed, and the two ludicrous charges of procuring abortions which had not been included in the trial but had been put over to the next session on the judge's direction after the verdict were left forever. No-one knew what the judge would have done, because he kept it a secret. Like so many in this story he is dead and in his case he took the sentence to the grave with him.

Ward's funeral at Mortlake Cemetery was attended by close family, his last girl-friend and his solicitor. The people who always wanted Ward and his girls at a party stayed away. But there was an enormous bouquet of one hundred white roses sent by twenty-one writers and artists, including John Osborne and Kenneth Tynan, with a card which said simply:

'To Stephen Ward,
a victim of British hypocrisy.'

Lewis was not at the funeral but he toasted the death. He held
his glass high and said 'Serve the bastard right.'

After that it was all downhill. Lord Denning reported
(blaming mainly Ward and exonerating everyone else with some
mild criticism) and his 70,000-word report sold 105,000 copies
on the first day. It was the reading matter of the moment with a
good strong narrative and plenty of spice as well as being a fair
account. Macmillan got prostate trouble and had to retire as
Prime Minister and Leader of the Tory party. His successor was
Lord Home, chosen in a mysterious and vicious Tory
blood-letting at the annual conference at Blackpool. He was an
honest, decent man but he had to take over a party that was
highly unpopular and regarded by many as having created a
society in which lax morals were far too prominent. He led them
to a very narrow defeat in 1964 which Wilson consolidated into
a sound majority two years later, with his cry of 'Thirteen
Wasted Years.'

In December 1963 Keeler was gaoled for nine months for
perjury in the Gordon trial. She had dropped a long way from
Cliveden and Profumo to spend Christmas in Holloway but she
was a survivor and is to this day. She is now a successful author.
Rice-Davies is too a successful author and actress and singer.

Lewis was was not able to capitalize on his incredible victory.
The Labour Party did not want to know him. The press would
not go near him.

He was left with his satisfaction and the memory of the 'ifs'
that worked so successfully in his favour: if he had not met
Keeler and she let slip the magic word Ward; if Profumo had
owned up instead of lying and suing which was why Macmillan
and his colleagues accepted his word; if the security forces had
not been sulking over Vassall and the gamekeeper jibe and
appointments kept and statements passed on, then it might have
been different.

As we know each of these points and others on their own were
important. Together they created disaster because the action of
one man pushing the small snowball started a course which
ruined Profumo and eventually cost the Tories the power of
government.

It was an achievement never equalled in British history and it was all because Lewis thought – wrongly – that Stephen Ward had slept with his wife the night she cried on his shoulder.

Of such small seeds is history made.

18

CONCLUSION

After the excitement surrounding Ward's death, the rest of the year was an anticlimax, ending with Lewis being arrested for driving while unfit through drink. It was pure Lewis at his worst. Mid-afternoon on 9 December 1963 near his home in St John's Wood, he bumped into the back of a van in traffic. The damage was minimal and the van driver was quite happy to exchange details and leave it at that. Not Lewis. He wanted the police called and for the accident to be sorted out at the police station and so two policemen arrived. They immediately smelt drink on his breath (tests later showed that he had had the equivalent of six and a half pints of beer or thirteen single whiskies) and on the way to the police station Lewis gave vent to his feelings in a loud voice. He said: 'If you accuse me of drinking I will lumber you,' and 'I'll bloody well lumber you. I've no occupation, I'm a spiv ... I've had a pint of beer, you bloody fools. I will not sign any document, I made all the laws in my time.' He added his view that all policemen were 'bloody fools'.

Two doctors examined him and made him do the tests, such as walking along a line, touching toes and nose to test co-ordination and balance, that were always carried out pre-breathalyser. They said he was drunk.

When he appeared at Clerkenwell magistrates' court in January he elected to go for trial and strongly denied the charge. He appeared at the London Sessions in June 1964 where he defended himself, pleading not guilty. His defence was simple: either the police were lying or he and his witnesses were and the duty sergeant's evidence was a 'fabric of untruth'.

Two of his witnesses were interesting. The first was his secretary-housekeeper, Mrs Stella Hayes, who became Stella

King after her marriage was dissolved and then Mrs Stella Lewis when she married him on 20 November 1968. She said he was sober when he left home and returned.

The second was his old friend Commander Arthur Townsend. Commanders in the Metropolitan police do not usually give evidence in drink-driving cases but there was a special reason this time. The commander had had a call on the morning of the accident from Lewis. Lewis said he had picked up some information on the grapevine that a very important public figure had been threatened with assassination. That kind of tip, from a man whose track record was exceptionally impressive, was not to be ignored. And when Lewis rang him, he had no reason to think he was the worse for drink.

The commander made no mention of the earlier help Lewis had given the police, such as the information that lit the inferno under Ward.

The questions and answers went like this:

Lewis said: 'Have I been helpful to the police?'

The commander replied: 'Yes, undoubtedly, on a matter of very considerable public importance.'

Lewis: 'There had been a threat made to a man of public importance?'

'Yes.'

Lewis: 'There was a threat of assassination?'

'Yes.'

But the commander did not elaborate, and no-one knows who the public figure was, and whether the plot to kill him really existed, and if it did, how it was foiled.

In his closing speech Lewis denied making the remarks the police attributed to him. He said they had been made up to make him sound pompous and stupid and attract the press. He was right. The case did attract the press and had good coverage but no-one linked him to Profumo and Ward.

The case lasted four days and the jury were out for only twenty minutes before they returned to find him guilty. He was fined £75, disqualified for eighteen months and ordered to pay 250 guineas costs, a heavy penalty which he brought on himself. He inevitably appealed, but it was turned down with one judge calling his behaviour in the police station as 'indescribable'.

It was very much a re-run of the motoring incident in 1951, when his persistence in having it referred to the Committee of

Privileges and his behaviour towards two young constables made him a marked man and led to the end of his parliamentary career.

This time his trial and fine did not matter. No-one was going to offer him any position in politics.

In October 1964 his beloved Labour party won power, creeping in with a majority of five. He celebrated because it was really he who had put them there, not that he was given any thanks. It must have been a wonderful feeling to know that you have achieved the downfall of a prime minister and a government which had run for thirteen years.

Then, in December, Lewis appeared in the newspapers for the last time. His libel action against the *Daily Mail* and the *Daily Telegraph* was finally settled. It was nothing like the sum he had been awarded three years before but it was still a large sum. It was announced on 17 December that he would receive £6,000 from each of the papers and his company (which was no longer trading) £5,000 from each, a total of £22,000. The papers waived their costs in the court of appeal and the House of Lords, amounting to about £10,000.

But this time Lewis was not a well man. Stella nursed him devotedly and he married her in November 1968 (two years after Labour had been given a majority of ninety-six by the country). He died in June 1969, from his heart condition.

He left over £70,000 in his will but that did not include the provision he had made for his daughter earlier. After personal bequests, including a lump sum and all his personal papers and possessions to Stella, he left the rest to found the John Lewis Memorial Trust with the income going to his widow but the capital going towards research by the British Heart Foundation. All the money went to the foundation when Stella died in 1984. He also recorded that he was leaving nothing else to charity, 'as throughout my life I have made generous contributions'.

There was an obituary in *The Times* which was a factual record of his life, ending by saying that Stella had been his secretary for eight years and that they had married shortly before his death. In the north there were warm tributes, even though he had not been an MP since 1951. It was, it was recalled in Bolton, because of the pact between the Tories and the Liberals not to oppose each other in the two Bolton divisions that Lewis's constituency fell to a Liberal.

He was remembered as a good MP who dealt with surgery cases at the rate of five thousand a year and was a champion of anyone who took a problem to him. He fought against bad housing conditions and was also against conscription. He would pursue any injustice that he found and was never afraid to speak out on behalf of those he thought were not being treated fairly. One Bolton man who knew Lewis for years said: 'He was an extraordinarily good MP, one of the best Bolton ever had and very popular with the people.'

It was a fair tribute. It was not one that those who had crossed him would give but how were the people of Bolton to know? And even if they did, it would have made no difference to his performance on their behalf. No one there ever crossed him.

SOURCES

The Denning report has been used as the marker for the dates and certain facts, particularly official records. Other material has come from contemporary reports and interviews with acquaintances of Lewis, Ward and other leading characters and from personal recollection and meetings.

Other sources are (chapter titles):

1 JOHN LEWIS: family background, parliamentary career, Bolton football disaster, Singapore court-martial, engagement and marriage – *The Times*, contemporary newspaper reports, Lewis's election manifesto and publicity details.
2 FIRST LIBEL: *The Times* Law Reports.
3 PRIVILEGE: *The Times* parliamentary reports. Court case from contemporary reports.
4 STEPHEN WARD: interviews and contemporary reports.
5 THE MULLALLY LIBEL CASE: *The Times* Law Reports.
6 DIVORCE: *The Times* and contemporary reports.
7 THE FIFTIES: Austin and Hamama High Court actions from *The Times* Law Reports.
8 PROFUMO AND KEELER: historical background from contemporary accounts.
9 THE LEWIS LIBEL CASE: *The Times* Law Reports.
10 TIME LAG: *The Times* contemporary reports.
11 1962: *The Times* Law Reports, *Queen* magazine.
12 THE SHOOTING: contemporary reports, *The Times* Law Reports.
13 OUT IN THE OPEN: contemporary reports.
14 THE SNOWBALL ROLLS ON: *The Times* Law Reports and Parliamentary reports. *Westminster Confidential*.
15 AVALANCHE: letter to Commander Townsend from Ward: *The Times* report of the trial of Stephen Ward.
16 THE END OF THE AFFAIR: *The Times* Parliamentary report.
17 VICTORY FOR LEWIS: trial reports: *The Times* Gordon appeal: *The Times*.
18 CONCLUSION: Lewis trial report: *The Times* Obituary: *The Times* and Bolton Library archives.

BIBLIOGRAPHY

Charlton, Warwick, *Stephen Ward Speaks* (Today Press, 1963)

Denning, Lord
> Lord Denning's Report 'to examine, in the light of the circumstances leading to the resignation of the former Secretary of State for War, Mr J.D. Profumo, the operation of the Security Service and the adequacy of their co-operation with the Police in matters of security, to investigate any information or material which may come to his attention in this connection and to consider any evidence there may be for believing that national security has been, or may have been, endangered.' (HMSO, 1963).

Irving, C. Hall, R. and Wallington, J., *Scandal '63: A Study of the Profumo Affair* (Heinemann, 1963)

Ivanov, Eugene, *The Naked Spy* (Blake, 1992)

Keeler, Christine, and Medley, George, *Sex Scandals* (Xanadu, 1985)

Keeler, Christine, and Fawkes, Sandy, *Nothing But* (New English Library, 1983)

Kennedy, Ludovic, *The Trial of Stephen Ward* (Gollancz, 1964)

Knightley, Phillip, and Kennedy, Caroline, *An Affair of State* (Guild Publishing, 1987)

Macmillan, Harold, *At the end of the Day* (Macmillan 1973)

Rice-Davies, Mandy, *The Mandy Report* (Confidential Publications, 1964)

Summers, Anthony and Dorril, Stephen, *Honeytrap* (Weidenfeld and Nicolson, 1987)

West, Nigel, *A Matter of Trust: MI5 1945 – 72* (Weidenfeld and Nicolson, 1982)

Wigg, Lord, *George Wigg* (Michael Joseph, 1972)

Young, Wayland, *The Profumo Affair: Aspects of Conservatism* (Penguin, 1963)

INDEX

Alexander, Field Marshal, 66
Argyll, Duke and Duchess, 149
Arran, Lord, 89
Astor, Lord 'Bill', 32, 63, 66, 67-70, 71,
    87, 89, 90, 100, 113, 116, 118–20,
    134, 147, 172, 173
Attlee, Clement (Lord), 20, 58
Austin, Herschel Lewis, 57, 58

Barry, Mr Justice, 58
Bass, John, 21
Bay of Pigs, 79
Beaverbrook, Lord, 36
Bell, Laurence, 153, 154
Bevan, Aneurin, 21, 23
Beyfus, QC, Gilbert, 48, 51, 57, 59
Birch, Nigel, 163, 168
Blake, George, 42
Bligh, Timothy, 150, 156, 157
Blunt, Anthony, 171
Bolton, 10, 11, 16, 17, 28, 185, 186
Bolton football disaster, 11, 12
Boothby, (Lord) Bob, 66, 170
Boyd, Leslie, 135
Brasenose College, Oxford, 65, 116
British Heart Foundation, 185
British Boxing Board of Control, 14, 16,
    50
Brook, Sir Norman (Lord), 75, 76
Brooke, Henry, 135–7, 144, 151
Brown, George, 106
Burge, James, 174, 175
Burrows, Det Sgt, 112, 139, 145, 152
Busse, John, 22
Butler, R.A., 62, 66, 137
Butler-Sloss, Mrs Justice, 86

Caccia, Sir Harold, 81
Castle, Barbara, 130, 131, 133, 135, 136,
    139
Chapman, Eddie, 55, 56
Chapman-Walker, Mark, 119
Christiansen, Arthur, 36, 37
Churchill, Sir Winston, 21, 23, 32, 60, 71

Churchill's, 56
City Fraud Squad, 72–4
Cliveden, 63, 65, 67, 69, 147
Clore, Charles, 58, 172
Coote, Sir Colin, 64
Cordingley, Police Constable, 25, 26
Crossman, Richard, 131, 134, 139
Cunnington, John, 59–61
    Marguerite, 59–61
Curtis-Bennett, QC, Derek, 40–4

Daily Express, 36, 37, 146
Daily Mail, 59, 72–5, 79, 95, 185
Daily Sketch, 132
Daily Telegraph, 32, 59, 72–5, 79, 95, 185
Deedes, (Lord) William, 137
Denning, Lord, 8, 83, 121, 128, 135, 138,
    170, 179
Dilhorne, Lord, 156
Director of Public Prosecutions, 122, 123,
    146, 147, 160
Dors, Diana, 31
Douglas-Home, Robin, 87
Driberg, Tom, 12, 38

East, Roy, 107–9
Eastham, Michael, 59
Eddowes, Michael, 97, 98, 146
Ede, Chuter, 21
Eden, Sir Anthony, 61
Edgecombe, John, 82, 93, 95–8, 100, 110,
    113, 115, 123, 127, 131, 132,
    143, 146
Edinburgh, Duke of, 20, 32
Edwards, John, 16
Edwards, Dennis Kennerly, 40–5
Eichmann, 32
Elwes, Dominic, 38
Equine Research Station, 61
Evening News, 74

Fairbanks, Douglas, 172
Farouk, King, 59
Faulks, Neville, 73, 95

Foster, Reg, 125
Friend, Tommy, 92

Gagarin, Yuri, 70, 76, 140
Gaitskell, Hugh, 62, 106, 131
Galbraith, Thomas, 91, 116, 118, 125
Gardiner, (Lord) Gerald, 17–19, 57
Gardner, Ava, 37
Getty, Paul, 32, 62
Giles, Carl, 162
Gillis, Bernard, 40
Goddard, Ltd, Theodore, 102, 118
Gordon, Lucky, 81, 82, 84, 96–8, 143, 149, 159, 177–8, 181
Griffith-Jones, Mervyn, 172-8
GRU, 71
Gulbenkian, Nubar, 62

Hailsham, Lord, 66, 159, 163
Hallett, Mr Justice, 17
Hamama (racehorse), 59–61
Hamilton, Denis, 31, 69, 129
Hare, John (Lord Blakenham), 157, 162
Harrow, 65, 116
Havers,
    Lord Chancellor Michael, 86
    Mr Justice, 86
Heath, Edward, 146, 170
Herbert, DCI Samuel, 112, 145, 152, 154
Hilbery, Mr Justice, 40, 45
Hobson, Sir John, 65, 116–18, 120
Hollis, Sir Roger, 75, 116, 144
Home, Lord, 81, 87, 89, 181
House of Commons: Committee, of Privileges, 24–6

Illustrated London News, 32
Ivanov, Captain Eugene,
    meets Ward, friendship/socializing, 63–5, 80, 81, 87, 110
    Cliveden, affair with Keeler, 68–71, 97, 111–2
    'turning', 76
    Cuban crisis, 88–90
    Lewis, 103–4, 115
    departure and aftermath, 118, 122, 132, 140, 143

Kassem, General, 64, 65, 71, 95
Kaye, Danny, 32
Keeler, Christine, 31, 75
    meets Profumo, Ivanov (affairs), 67–71, 76, 77, 87
    nuclear warhead question, 77

meets Gordon/Edgecombe, 81, 82, 87, 93
    shooting, tells Lewis, 96–105
    talks to *Sunday Pictorial*, 110–13
    talks to police, 113, 114
    legal discussions, 115–26
    Edgecombe trial: on holiday, 126
    named and aftermath, 127–41
    investigation of Ward, 145–6
    bomb question, 148
    Gordon, 149
    Ward talks, 150–1
    Profumo resigns, 155–7
    Gordon in court and appeal, 159, 177–9
    Ward trial, 171–80
    jailed, 181
Kendall, Kay, 29
Kennedy, John (US President), 79, 88, 97, 147, 170
Kennedy, Paddy, 28, 56
KGB, 14, 71
Khruschchev, Russian leader, 64, 79, 88, 90
Kuwait, 64, 66, 71, 91

Labour Party, 19, 78, 87, 100, 101, 146, 149, 163, 181, 185
Latey, John, 48
Lavadin, Derby winner, 59
Lawton, (Lord) Fred, 57
Lewis, John,
    background/MP, 8–12
    first libel, 16–19
    Committee of Privileges, 20–7
    Marylebone court, 21–2
    loses seat, 28
    cause of hatred, 32–7
    wife leaves, 35–7
    Mullally libel, 35–45
    divorce, 35, 36, 39, 40, 43, 46–54
    social life, 55–7
    sued by Austin, 57–8
    Hamama case, 59–61
    sues *Daily Mail/Daily Telegraph*, 59, 72–5
    snowball runs, 77, 79, 84, 126
    Court of appeal, 85–6
    Lords appeal/result, 95, 141–2
    Keeler talks, 98–102, 110
    tells Wigg/Townsend, 103–10
    hatred for Ward, 107–8
    putting in the poison, 113, 127–9, 134, 141, 143, 147, 149, 152–3, 159

Commons debate, 163, 165
victory over Ward, 169, 174, 179–81
driving case, 183–5
libel settlement/death, 185
Lewis, Joy,
engagement, marriage, 14
talks to Ward, 33–4
leaves husband, 35–6, 38–9
divorce, 46–54
Lewis, Stella,
secretary/marriage, 183–5
Lloyd, Selwyn, 62
Longford, Lord, 90
Lonsdale, Gordon, 62, 63
Lyell, Mr Justice, 132

MacArthur, General Douglas, 66
Macleod, Ian, 137, 159, 162
Macmillan, Harold, 8, 62, 66, 83, 87, 89,
91, 98, 119–21, 122, 123, 135,
136, 139, 144, 146, 148, 150, 151,
154–8, 161–70, 181
Macmillan, Lady Dorothy, 170
Marshall, Mr Justice, 171–80
MI5, 68, 70, 75, 79, 84, 114, 126, 174
MI6, 125
Milford Haven, Marquis of, 20
Mills, John (club owner), 56
Milmo, Helenus, 59
Mulholland, Brendan, 125
Mullally, Freddy, 28, 33
Ward and Mrs Lewis, 33–4
Lewis hatred for Ward, 34–6
background, 36
Lewis sues for libel, 35–46
Lewis wins, 47
Lewis accuses him of adultery/divorce
case, 48–55
Murray's Club, 69

National Coal Board, 37, 58
News of the World, 110, 119, 141
Nicholson, Sir Godfrey, 80, 81, 89, 151
Norris, Fred, 16
Novotny, Mariella, 82, 83, 108

O'Brien, Barry R., 149
Oliphant on Horses, 60
Osborne, John, 180

Pack of Lies, A, 62
Paget, QC MP, Reginald, 17, 18, 21, 23,
24, 26
Pakistan, President of, 65–8

Parachute Regiment, Malaya, 12,
13
Parker, Lord, 177, 178
Parkin, Ben, 107, 132–3
Paull, Gilbert, 40, 44, 48, 60, 61
Pearce, Lord Justice, 85
Penkovsky, Colonel Oleg, 68
Philby, Kim, 71, 146, 170, 171
Phillips, Morgan, 58
Poole, Lord, 162
Portland Spy Ring (Lonsdale, Krogers,
Gee Houghton), 62, 63
Profumo, John/Jack, 8, 9, 82, 97
background, 65–6
Cliveden, meets Keeler, 65–71, 87
sees Cabinet Secretary, 75–7
ends affair, letter, 77, 79, 84, 91
Blue Water missile, 87
Kuwait debate/Wigg, 92–4
Keeler tells Lewis/others, 100–6,
111–13
denials, 116–26
timelag, 127, 129–30
named in House and personal state-
ment, 131–41
sues, 148
Ward talks, 150–1
end of pretence, 154–8
resignation, aftermath/debate, 159–69,
181

Profumo, Valerie,
marriage, loyal wife, 65
Cliveden, 67
personal statement, 136–8, 140

Queen magazine, 87
Queen Mother, 140

Rachman, Peter, 31, 69, 84, 95, 129
Radcliffe, Lord, 63
Rawlinson, (Lord) Peter, 116, 118, 137
Redmayne, Martin, 117, 120, 121–3, 136,
137, 139, 156, 157
Rees-Davies, William, 116, 120
Rice-Davies, Mandy, 3, 69, 82, 84, 95,
96, 112, 113, 128, 131, 132, 133,
152, 171–3, 180, 181
Richards, Sir Gordon, 57, 60
Richards, Morley, 36, 37
Rickaby, Billy, 60
Rickard, Norman, 107
Robinson, Sugar Ray, 14
Roth, Andrew, 130
Rubber Improvement Ltd, 72–6, 86

Ryan, Kathleen, 37

Sachs, Mr Justice, 46–54, 177
Salmon, Mr Justice, 73–5
Saunders, Geoffrey, 16
Savundra, Dr Emil, 172
Shinwell, Emanuel, 153
Shute, Nevil (On the Beach), 88
Silverman, Sydney, 23–4
Simpson, Sir Joseph, 141, 145
Sinatra, Frank, 32
Special Branch, 114, 115
Star The, Belgravia, 28, 56
Starritt, Sir John, 109
Sunday Pictorial/Mirror, 36, 110, 115

Taylor, Elizabeth, 32
Theisger, Mr Justice, 132
Thomas, Rowland QC, 21
Times, The, 148, 160, 163, 185
Tousson, Prince, 59–61
Townsend, Cdr. Arthur, 106–10, 113,
        129, 141, 145, 147, 152–4, 160,
        169, 184
Turpin, Randolph, 14
Two Thousand Guineas, 60
Tynan, Kenneth, 186

Vassall, William, 63, 88, 95, 116, 133,
        144, 152, 181
Vigar, Alan, 107

Wakefield, Sir Wavell, 151
Ward, Stephen
    introduction, 8, 9, 20
    upbringing, background, 28–32
    shoulder for Joy, 33–4, 45
    divorce: Lewis, 50, 54
    Lewis's hatred, 55
    meets Ivanov, 63–5
    Cliveden party, 67–71
    Profumo, 76, 77

    talks with Foreign Office, 80–1
    social life, 82–4, 87
    Cuba, 88–90
    shooting: Edgecombe, 97–100
    Lewis tells Wigg, 103–5
    Lewis hatred, 107, 108, 109, 114, 115,
        147
    Police and vice, 112, 113
    threat of publicity, 115, 116, 119, 120,
        123, 124, 125
    Press and Lewis's hatred, 127–9, 136
    Profumo statement, 140–1
    sees Wigg, 143–4
    investigation begins, 144–5
    Wigg/Lewis dossier, 148
    fights when trapped, 149–53
    Townsend letter, 152–4
    fights on, 155
    arrest, trial, 160, 170–9
    death, 179–82
Warner, Suzanne, 36, 50
Watkinson, Harold, 64
Westminster Confidential, 129–30
White, Sir Dick, 116, 141, 144, 145, 155
Whitemore, Hugh, 62
Wigg, (Lord) George, 27, 57, 65, 84, 91
    school/background, 77–8
    Kuwait operation, 92–4
    tip to watch Profumo, 92–4
    Lewis tells him, 103–6, 109, 128
    raises it in House, 128–36
    anger at Profumo, 141
    doctored divorce paper, 143
    sees Ward, 143–4
    Bell subpoena, 153
    Victory, 155, 168–9, 177
Wilson, (Lord) Harold, 38, 91, 106, 131,
        144, 146–51, 154–6, 163–5, 181
Winterton, Earl, 23
Wyndham, John, 119, 120, 122

Yugoslavia, King of, 32